Volume 1

ART &

Center for Advanced Study in the Visual Arts

National Gallery of Art
Washington

Distributed by
Yale University Press
New Haven and London

Kaira M. Cabañas, series editor

ART & HISTORIES

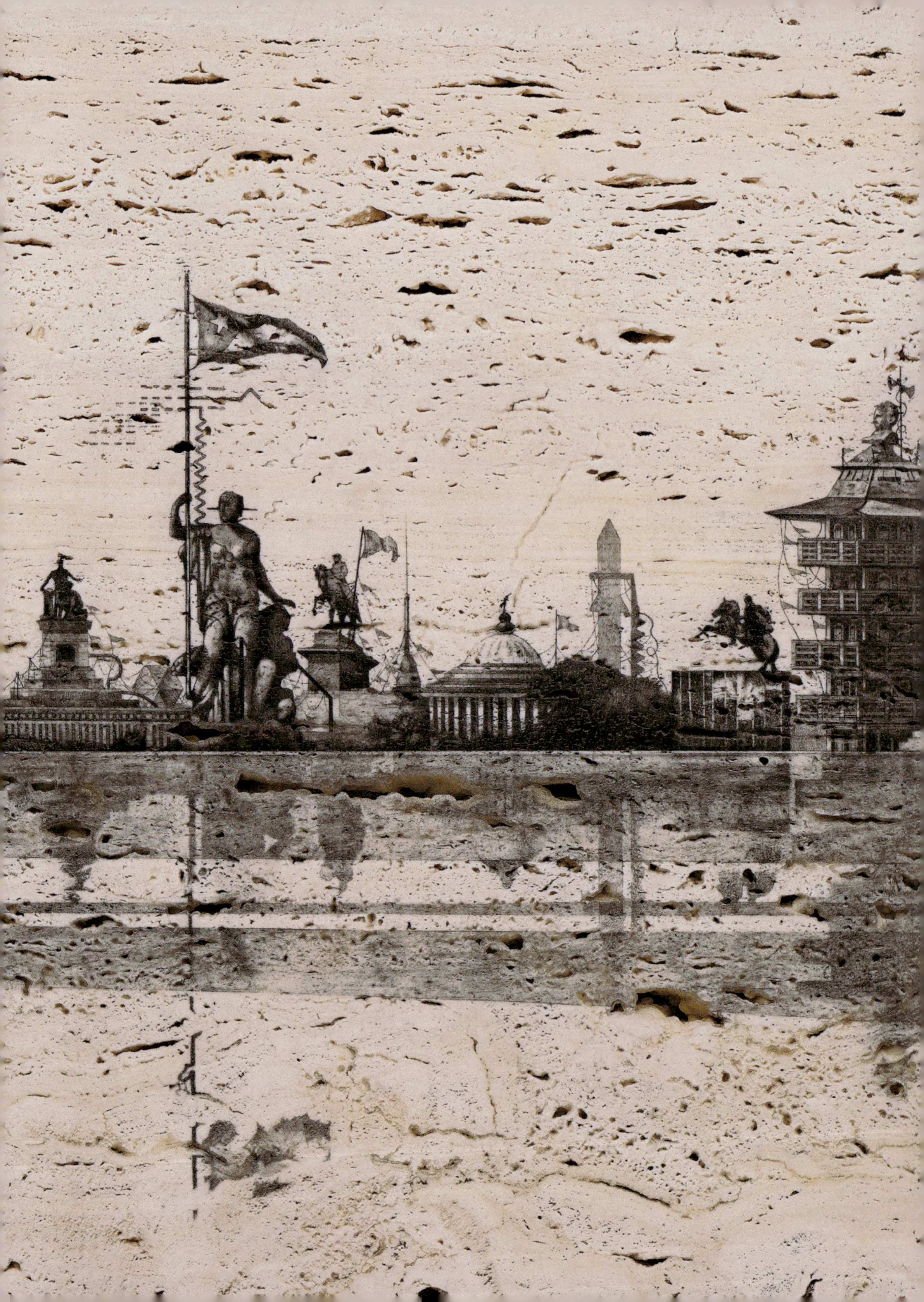

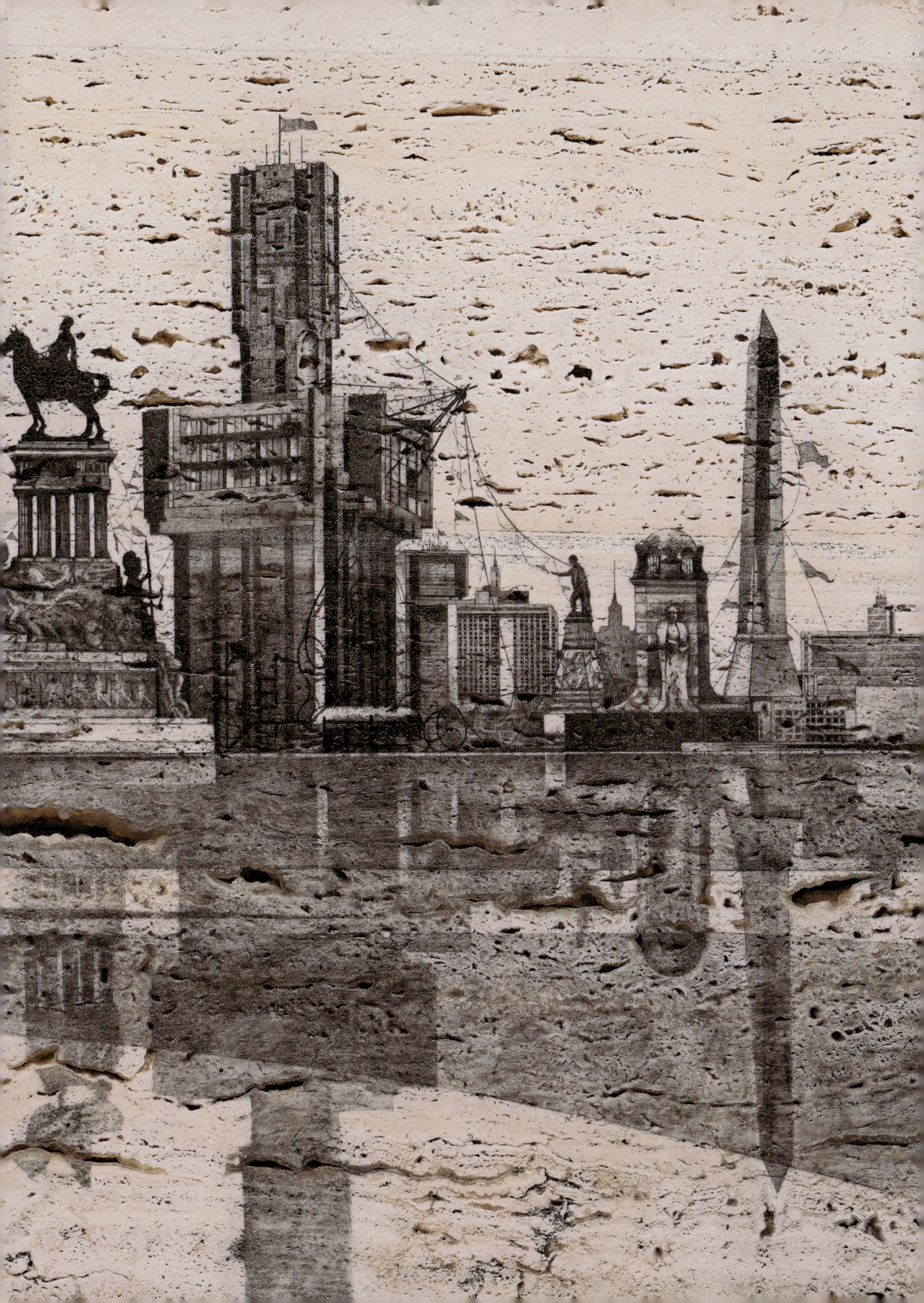

CONTENTS

VOLUME 1

Steven Nelson
Dean, Center for Advanced Study in the Visual Arts

FOREWORD

Shortly after Kaira M. Cabañas arrived at the Center for Advanced Study in the Visual Arts in early 2023 as associate dean for academic programs and publications, I asked her to survey our publishing program with an eye toward how it could connect to the Center's broadening vision of scholarship and its relationship to different audiences as well as to the National Gallery's mission to expand access to art, the production of knowledge, and creativity. Armed with years of publishing experience and an international network of interlocutors, within a couple of months Kaira presented a brilliant concept and plan for Art &. I am thrilled to witness the publication of its inaugural volume: *Art & Histories*.

As Kaira deftly explains in her preface to the series, Art & takes as its primary goal the deepening of public understanding of the arts and why they matter. This series engages contributors from multiple disciplines, and it brings together scholars, critics, artists, and more on an issue of mutual interest: to expand our comprehension of the arts and the ways they work in both historical and contemporary contexts. I am very excited to see the directions this series will take as it continues.

Many people contributed to bringing *Art & Histories* to fruition, and I deeply appreciate their support. Gary Calcagno and Sarah Battle expertly supported Kaira, coordinating the Editorial Advisory Board as well as the volume's authors. Helen Tangires, Sarah Bohannan, and Nathalie Meza managed the publication's budget and administration. *Art & Histories* is the hallmark of deep collaboration with the National Gallery's Office of Brand Strategy and Publishing. I thank Peggy Martin, chief brand officer and publisher, for her enthusiasm and support. Emily Zoss served as managing editor. Magda Nakassis was project and copy editor. Extra Official led the creative direction and design, coordinated by Brad Ireland. Christina Wiginton took charge of production.

I am grateful to the authors for their wonderful contributions, and to Glexis Novoa, whose artwork visually explores the nexus between art and histories. I thank the Editorial Advisory Board for their dedication, generosity, and intellectual agility. I am deeply indebted to Kaira for her clear and expansive vision for Art &, a series that will dovetail beautifully with the Center's commitment to bringing together different forms of expertise, to engaging wider audiences through publications, and to broadening how we understand art and its work in the world.

Kaira M. Cabañas

I am honored to introduce the new book series from the Center for Advanced Study in the Visual Arts: Art &. As a series, Art & is an invitation to think about art together with the issues it shapes through material and imaginative expressions. The ampersand in the title is intentional both typographically and conceptually. By foregrounding & in the title, the series signals how art does not stand alone but is always already entangled with people, ideas, materials, networks, and communities. Accordingly, for each volume the series title is paired with a specific subject—for example, Histories, Water, Abilities.

In structure and ambition, Art & aims to be iterative and expansive; to be driven by ideas in relation to art's histories; to displace cultural and epistemological hierarchies; to link past and present, bringing historical knowledge to bear on the present and future. Offering multiple points of entry through varied formats—for example, the inaugural volume includes an artist commission, an Openings section with first-person narratives, and a group of scholarly essays—the series engages aesthetic and cultural debates that situate research on the arts at the intersection of various disciplines, including art and architecture, film, literature, curatorial and museum studies, and the arts of performance.

In writing about how to make Chinese art history more dynamic in light of global art history's development in "the West," Wu Hung provides important insights for how one might think about the study of all art moving forward. He writes,

> Here are two initial suggestions: First, although much progress has been made, art history in the West remains a conglomeration of regional and national art histories. Historians of Chinese art should work with their colleagues to gradually transform this system into a new, *three-dimensional structure*

1
Wu Hung, response to "A Questionnaire on Global Methods" by George Baker and David Joselit (*October* 180 [2022]: 60) (emphasis mine).

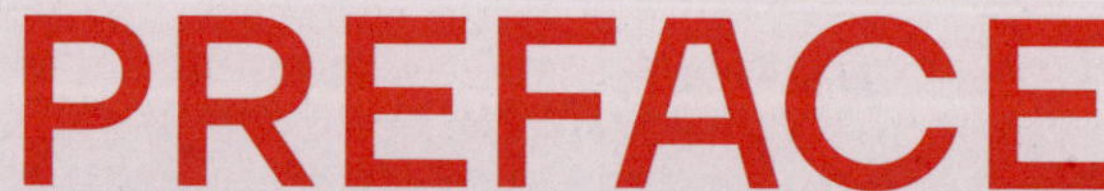

PREFACE

braiding multilinear, "vertical" national art histories into layered *"horizontal" narratives* and comparative projects....Based on actual historical connections and comparative analyses, this three-dimensional art-historical knowledge *will further reshape institutions*, including academic departments, research institutes, and museums. In this sense, the development of global art history is both *epistemic and organizational*.[1]

Though the term "global" is often (and paradoxically) understood as referring to all things non-Western, the horizontal, epistemic, and organizational transformation Wu Hung describes resonates with and takes up residence within the structure and organization of Art &, and the research and writing it enables and supports.

By orienting this new book series toward issues as a form of three-dimensional art history, Art & aspires to be agile and responsive, addressing key contemporary questions through nonhierarchical understandings of what counts as culture. In this way, Art & serves as a platform to expand art's histories in order to account for, and be responsible to, shifting frameworks of recognition for the arts and creativity. The series engages topics not only at the level of representation but also at the level of institutional and community dynamics, which yield various visual and sensory outcomes that empower multiple narratives. Consequently, Art & deliberately engages a project of epistemic delinking.[2] The series aims to foreground the epistemological, aesthetic, and material problematics of art in order to embrace "pluri-versality as [a] universal project leading toward a world in which many worlds will co-exist."[3] Rather than a disciplinary management of art history, with its recurrent institutional patterns and associations based on time period and geography, Art & instead aims to bring forth other knowledges about the arts, charting their role in the world and in world-making.

2
Walter Mignolo, "DELINKING: The Rhetoric of Modernity, the Logic of Coloniality and the Grammar of De-Coloniality," in "Globalization and De-Colonial Thinking," ed. Walter Mignolo with Arturo Escobar, special issue, *Cultural Studies* 21, no. 2 (March 2007): 449–514. I use the phrase "epistemic delinking" in this context to speak to the geopolitics of knowledge production in relation to art history (in which "the West" often maintains discursive power) in order to actively delink certain patterns/associations, including (1) disciplinary notions like field/subfield (which implies a hierarchy in which "subfield" is often marked as non-Western) and (2) the alignment of time period and geography, which produces the effect of siloed specializations.

3
Mignolo, "DELINKING," 72.

TO SERIES

Philosopher Karen Barad is an important reference for thinking about epistemic transformation and how one comes to "know" the things one knows. Expanding on the lessons of quantum physics and the philosophical insights of Niels Bohr, Barad affirms how "the very act of measurement produces determinate boundaries and properties of 'things,'" acknowledging that scientific observation does not represent but rather *produces* its object of study within a continual process of "cutting together-apart."[4] Her keen focus on the ways the world is configured and reconfigured (and how certain "things" come to matter) demands that attention be paid to the politics and ethics of knowledge production. When such ideas are engaged from the perspective of histories of art, one begins to practice a different materialization of art's histories, informed by research in the humanities writ large (e.g., cultural, ethnic, race, gender, and critical disability studies, as well as environmental, medical, and public humanities). In so doing, Art & enacts a vision for the study of art in which many worlds and ways of knowing can coexist, fostering a more dynamic intellectual landscape.

When thinking about the constitution of the Art & Editorial Advisory Board (EAB), I chose, with the support of Steven Nelson, to provide space for emerging scholars to deliberate the selection of authors and topics, and thus inform the discussions captured in these pages. The choice of emerging scholars resonates with a recent observation by artist Mickalene Thomas: "I think it's important as artists to create space for others who are coming forward so they have the same opportunities."[5] Luke Fidler, Shawon Kinew, Rachel Silveri, Igor Simões, and Adedoyin Teriba each contribute multiple research interests and methodological approaches, embracing sculpture and abolition, craft and the everyday, historiography and racialization, and architecture and folklore, among other pairings and entanglements. Together, we agreed to include an engaging mix of emerging

4
"Interview with Karen Barad," in *New Materialism: Interviews and Cartographies*, ed. Rick Dolphijn and Iris van der Tuin (Open Humanities Press, 2012), 62, 52. See also Karen Barad, *Meeting the Universe Halfway: Quantum Physics and the Entanglement of Matter and Meaning* (Duke University Press, 2007).

5
Mickalene Thomas, cited in Stephen Mooallem, "Maria Grazia Chiuri, Carrie Mae Weems, and Mickalene Thomas on Their Most Important Work," *Harper's Bazaar*, April 24, 2023.

and esteemed scholars in each volume. In our first year of convenings (2023–2024), each EAB member was an assistant or adjunct professor working at a different institution of higher learning, both public and private; two members are from the Global South. Center staff Gary Calcagno and Sarah Battle were also essential. Through their commitment, rigor, and nuanced considerations in our ongoing discussions, each brought the "&" in Art & alive, allowing it to signify "transformative expansion rather than mere addition or juxtaposition."[6]

Beyond the academy, Art & aspires to deepen public understanding of art and why art matters. Authors are encouraged to appeal to both general and specialized audiences and are invited to act on their own inspiration, to write in ways that are both methodologically and creatively meaningful. Accordingly, central to the EAB conversations was a deep commitment to accessibility. The print edition of Art & employs a thoughtful design that prioritizes a smaller and more portable book, legible type, high-contrast colors, generous line spacing, and matte paper. It also democratizes access to innovative art by hosting artist projects specifically designed for its pages. Art & is simultaneously published in a free ebook version—through a special open-access agreement with Yale University Press—that includes descriptive alternative text for images. Finally, our series intentionally includes multiple voices, topics, and writing styles that embody multiple ways of being and thinking, as well as practicing research on the arts. To this end, the volume's Openings section is imagined as a space for writers to reflect on how and why they came to study art (or, if they choose, to reflect on teaching and arts writing). I believe that telling stories of the unforeseen paths that led some to study art can enable others—who might otherwise feel unwelcome in art history—to creatively imagine how they might approach such scholarly work and make the study of art their own.

6
Luke Fidler, email message to author, December 15, 2023.

OPENINGS

“where tenderness is possible”

Lisa Gail Collins

June 15, 2024

Dear Hayden, Harrison, Maddy, Toby, Hannah, Jonathan, Natalia, Lauren, Louisa, Willow, Sadie, Maggie, Ava, Lila, Leo, Grace, Tilden, Olivia, Arden, Becca, and Zola,

I hope summer is taking the forms you need and shapes you desire!

It's mid-June, graduation and reunion are over, and during this slowed time I've been finding myself reveling in memories of our contemporary art class—Art, Urgency & Everyday Life—and reflecting on why our time together was so special for me.

This much I know is true: it was an absolute gift to be and grow with you; in your wise, kind, and courageous presence, my heart and brain considerably increased capacity.

In this open letter—a tiny, partial thank you—I'd like to share some reflections on the semester we spent together exploring how a wide range of US-based creators are grappling with urgent issues of our time. By putting these thoughts on the page, my hope is to offer a window into how I've been making meaning from my fond memories of our time together, and to share how I grew alongside you.

Enormous heartfelt thanks to Zola Simone Sullivan and Erika deVries for generously sharing their vital artwork, which continually stirs my soul and guides me on.

First, despite reflection, I'm still unclear how we found ourselves on the third floor of Taylor Hall.

My best guess is we are all art-minded, curious, and motivated by justice, and we gathered with a shared sense that immersing ourselves in the works and words of living artists with social practices might inspire, support, and guide us as we try to make our way in the world during this wrenching time of wars, forced migrations, hunger, homelessness, pandemics, and ecological disasters. My sense, too, is we were also seeking our own kind of practice space where we could think, critically and creatively, along with socially engaged artists and art projects by exploring their acts and ideas, practices and processes, materials and modes of making, and failures and possibilities—as well as our own.

Put a little differently, what I think we held in common was a desire for a place to practice world-building—the hopeful work of bringing future histories into being—rooted in, and sourced by, creativity and imagination coupled with conscience and courage. And perhaps, too, we gathered with a dawning realization that during this agonizing era of compounding crises, art and artists—including the creators and makers who are ourselves—were what we needed.

So, there it seems we were, the twenty-two of us, in a dark screening room with a tiny air purifier in the corner, trying collectively to figure out: What exactly is this thing called socially engaged, social practice, activist, and/or community-centered art? Where does it come from, who makes it, who is it for, how does it work, and what can it do? And what are some ways this participatory practice—often woven within struggles for justice and healing—is defined and deployed?

At heart, we were wondering and asking aloud: What is art capable of?

In our search for answers, we divided into collaborative working groups organized around specified issues of urgency (e.g., hunger, shelter, war, borders, debt,

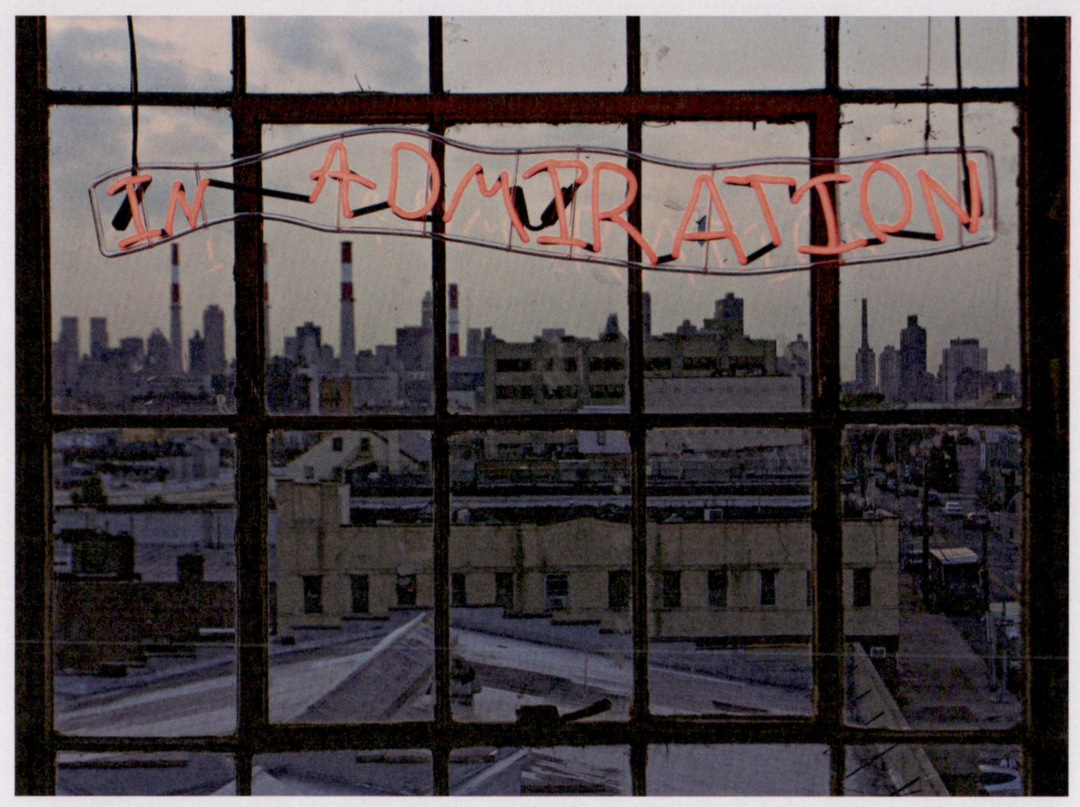

Erika deVries, *In Admiration*, 2010, neon sculpture, approximately 3.7 × 12.8 m, private collection

Erika deVries, *The Weather (Big Emotions)*, 2023, large-scale neon sculpture with metal framing, approximately 5.5 × 6.1 m, Headstone Gallery, Kingston, New York

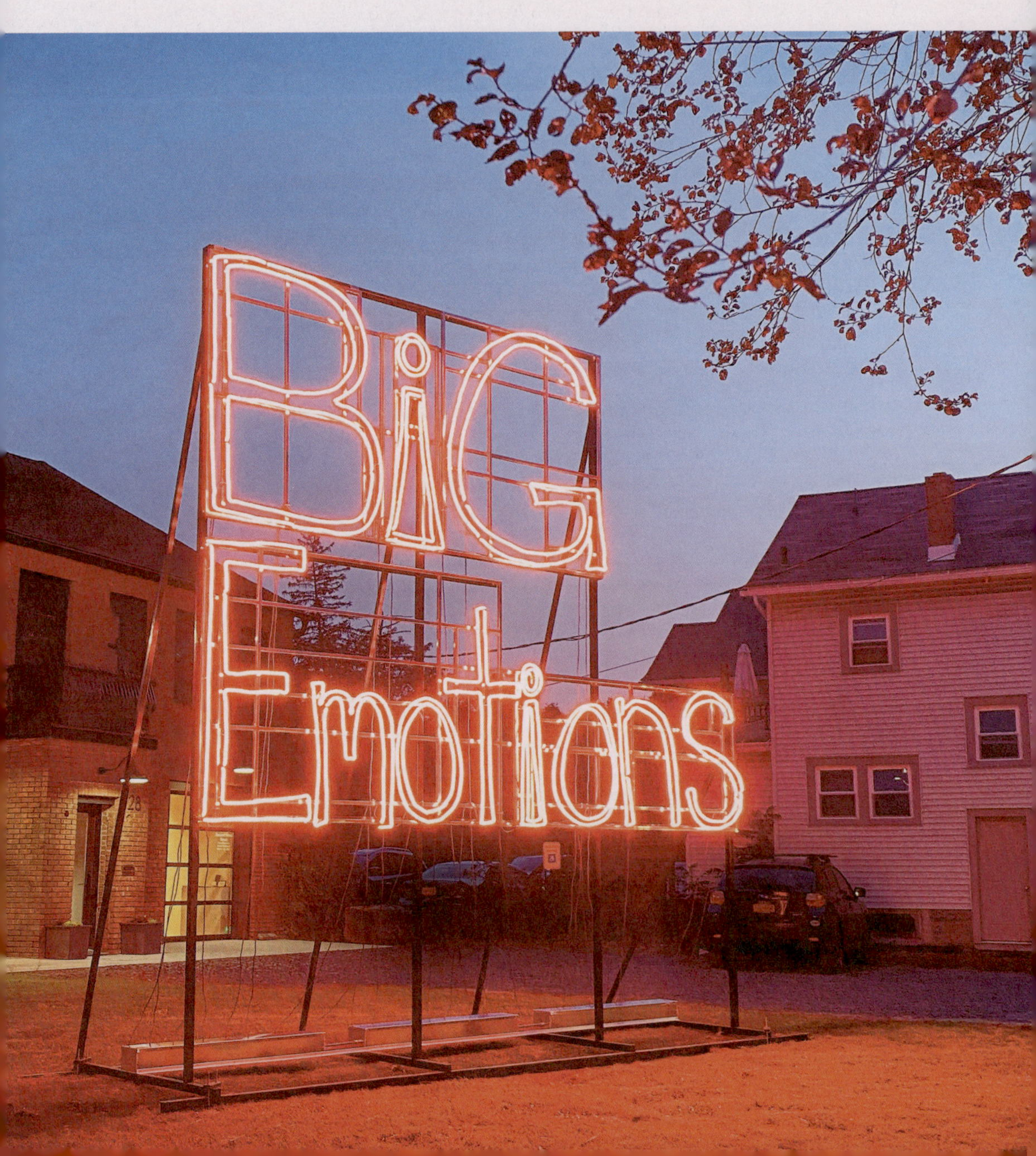

dis/ability, carcerality, climate crisis), each group tasked with deepening their knowledge of the subject, discovering and researching artists and art projects grappling with the intersectional issue at hand, and sharing their findings creatively. Without question the days you presented your findings were my favorite, as I was continually inspired (and frequently elated!) by the thought, effort, and care you put into your interdisciplinary research; the lasting questions you posed; and the truly exemplary ways you modeled collaboration.

Informed by your rich research, our searching and wide-ranging conversations, and continued thought, here's my best effort at answering the core question of our class:

Genuine engagement with the works and words of living artists with a social practice encourages us to make sense of, and have hope for, the world. And it does so across the continuum of time, asking (and sometimes urging) us to participate in making meaning of what was, what is, and what can be. Collectively, the artists' offerings create and hold space for us to reckon honestly with the past (e.g., deciding what to mourn, what to honor, what to end, what to leave behind, what to build on, and what to carry forward); to understand our present and to see the ways it's shaped by our past; and to imagine and try out loving and livable futures.

It's art, in essence, that reminds us of the journey we're on—living history as it is happening—and helps us determine its shape. Your collaborative research on creative projects (often made in or in relation to the US, given the scope of our class and my limited knowledge) and our generous exchange of ideas revealed this time and time again.

I regret I didn't set up a way for you to benefit from each other's writings. Next time you see me, please remind me of the easiest way to do that! In the meantime, here's a partial list of the artists and collectives who were richly engaged as thought partners, muses, and guides within our class. Retroactive extra credit for pursuing the work of creators new to you!

Sonya Clark, Tania Bruguera, Rick Lowe, Stephanie Syjuco, Cannupa Hanska Luger, Mary Mattingly, Chinatown Art Brigade, MASS Design Group, Nick Cave, Maria Gaspar, Jeffrey Gibson, Naima Green, Christine Sun Kim, Dread Scott, Finnegan Shannon, Amanda Phingbodhipakkiya, Oliver Herring, Judy Baca, Ai Weiwei, New Red Order, Ken Gonzales-Day, Amanda Williams, Tommy Kha, Shirin Neshat, Sable Elyse Smith, Young Joon Kwak, Abigail DeVille, Guadalupe Maravilla, Titus Kaphar, Riva Lehrer, Tanya Aguiñiga, Jesse Krimes, Jaune Quick-to-See Smith, Michael Rakowitz, Kelli Rae Adams, Azikiwe Mohammed, Marie Watt, Hank Willis Thomas, Favianna Rodriguez, Theaster Gates, Sasha Velour, LaToya Ruby Frazier.

One connective thread I see within this extraordinary list is that each artist, in their own way, asks us to face history.

Some press us to confront the truths and injustices of the past.
Some bring hard—often still hurting—histories to light.
Some carry forward, and grow, legacies of survival, resistance, and hope.

Some invite us to question what exactly history is made of and from.
Some put history in dialogue with memory.[1]

Some reveal ways histories have produced our present.
Some show how the past lives on inside us.

Some remind us we are all actors in history.
Some call on us to consider where we want to stand when history is written.

Some connect us with stories that help us heal.

1
On the nature of this dialogue, Agha Shahid Ali's words continue to capture my imagination. In "Farewell," a poem concerning war, displacement, (post) colonialism, and his yearning for the Kashmir of his childhood, the poet writes: "Your history gets in the way of my memory." Agha Shahid Ali, "Farewell," in *The Country Without a Post Office* (Norton, 1997).

Some open doors, all at once, to new ways of thinking
and ancient ways of knowing.
Some offer space to imagine other possible worlds.

And some face us firmly forward—toward future
histories—and encourage us to become the
ancestors our descendants deserve.

Activist/organizer and scholar Angela Davis reminds us that "Art helps us to find our way into new dimensions. Art helps to give expression to what might be considered impossible in the world that is. It shows us the possibility of a new world."[2] Her wise words concerning creativity and consciousness are especially apt here, for the socially engaged art projects we immersed ourselves in offered a range of realms to explore how things were, are, and can be. Our open-eyed engagement with works and words of living artists with social practices offered additional gifts as well, including an expansive tool kit tailored to our impossible time, one filled with creative strategies for surviving and thriving, grieving and mourning, engaging and resisting, organizing and protesting, naming and reframing, advocating and amplifying, tending and repairing, resting and healing, and imagining and dreaming.

Access to these teeming "dimensions" that art makes possible (and of which Davis speaks), including a generative, critical tool kit of creative strategies and resources, came to inform our own social practices. It's as if thinking alongside the artists and bearing witness to their bravery, ingenuity, and commitments to healthy communities and relations strengthened our own. And to my great delight (and relief), instead of passing viruses among ourselves in our windowless room, creativity, courage, and care spread everywhere.

It was an honor to be in your company. Each of you was entirely integral to the practice space we created within our classroom and beyond—please know you are

2
Angela Davis, interview by Erin Aubry Kaplan, Center for the Study of Political Graphics, Los Angeles, published in *Autumn Awakening* 18, no. 2 (2011).

always welcome back! Here, to close, I'd like to share my memories of just two of our class meetings as examples of how I grew alongside you.

You'll no doubt remember this scene:

It was a dreary, overcast day near the end of the semester and Tilden, Olivia, and Maddy (the group working on "Climate Crisis") walked into class and asked us to grab our jackets and journals, for we were heading outside. Eagerly wondering what the future held, we promptly followed them out of Taylor Hall and to the short winding trail that crosses the stream near Sunset Lake. Once gathered at the trailhead, they asked us to join them in walking silently along the marshy path while listening, really listening, to nature's songs and sounds. And so, we followed their lead, walking single file and, if my memory holds, somewhat solemnly like we were approaching someplace sacred. Then when we met again at the trail's end, we were encouraged to note our experiences with listening-while-walking in our journals. At this point, it started to rain lightly, and as none of us seemed to mind, the collaborators invited us to retrace our steps, to trace the trail again, but this time with a focus on our sense of sight and looking-while-walking. And we all did just that, filled with marvel and delight.

Although I'd taken this trail countless times before, our guided experience was transformative for me. And I knew it then, for I carefully dried and saved my notes from that day. They, in part, say:

grounding awe/calming wonder
slow steps/quick birds
sinking into self/melting into mud
life is loud! absorb. drink it in
invited + united
this nature walk is the antidote to (eco)anxiety

That silent walk was like slow, revelatory magic. Like a mash-up of reflection, movement, and prayer. As I walked

Artist statement →
Taking each step with gratitude. These are wearable ephemeral shoe stamps meant to capture and highlight the impressions our bodies leave on the Earth as we exist. With each step we take, something is left behind. With these shoes each step sends love and intention into the ground, thanking nature for providing us support and constructing our being.

Zola Simone Sullivan, *All My Love, All My Body*, 2023, ephemeral shoe stamps, dimensions variable, Vassar College campus

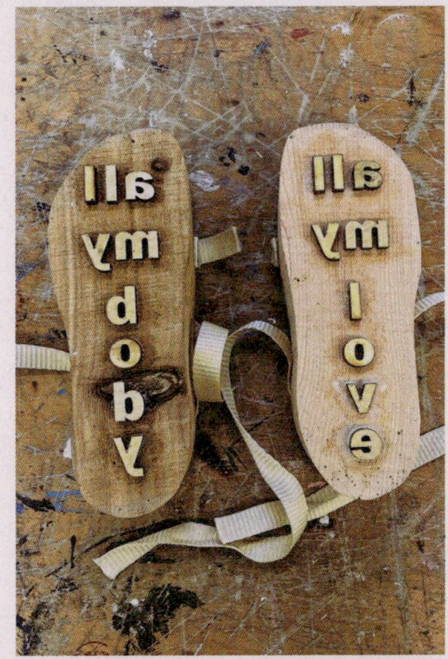

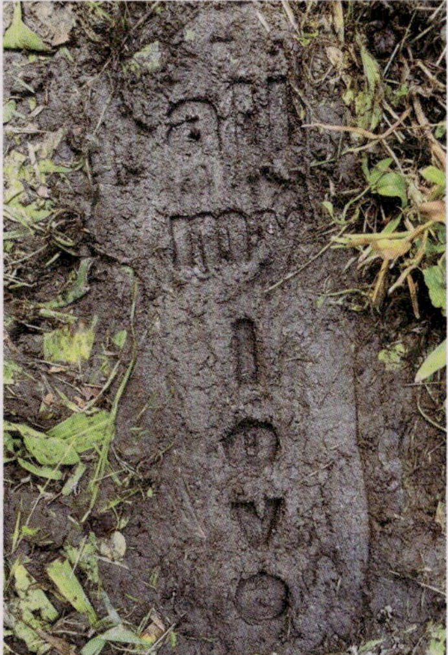

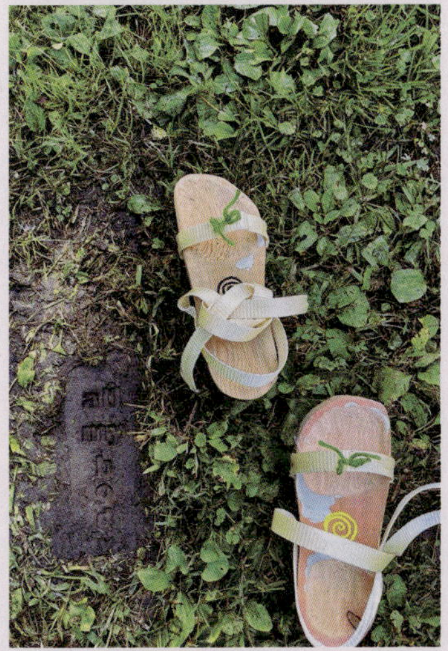

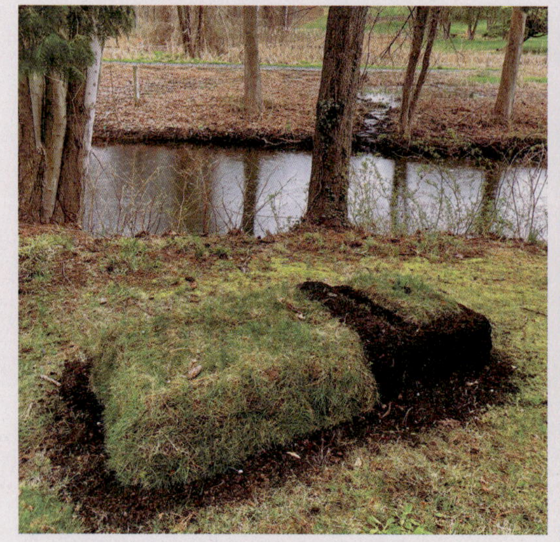

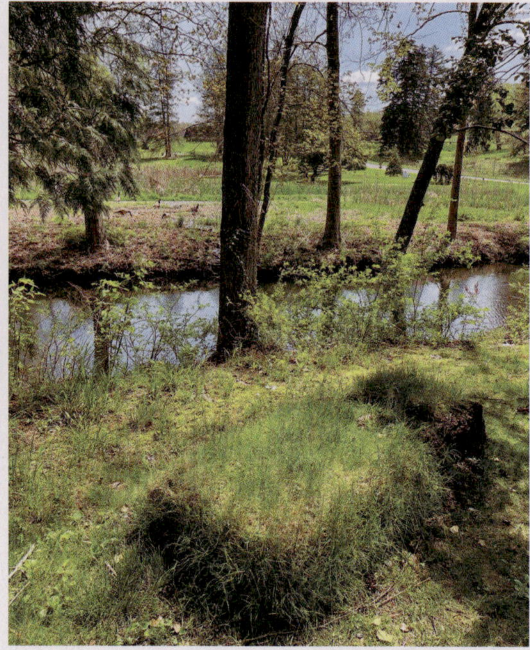

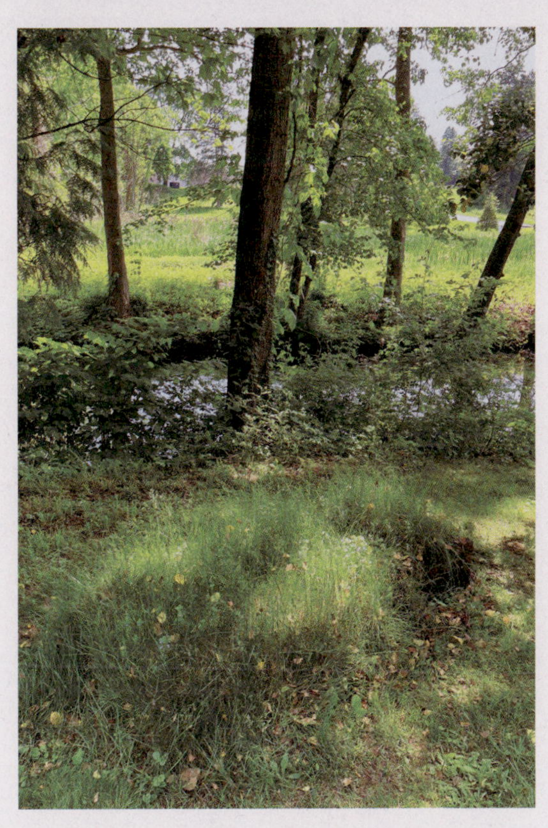

Zola Simone Sullivan, *Warm Grass*, 2024, ephemeral work, Vassar College campus

that path at my own pace, noticing what I noticed by way of sight and sound, a/the world was revealed, and it was sublime. I felt present, at ease, and connected to my inner instruction and the natural world. And interconnected with all of you. Rain-fed and breath-led, we were out of doors together, trying out this precious practice of listening and looking and sharing in wonder and awe. This embodied, participatory practice you shared was a wonderful gift, as it enabled us to feel more connected to the earth, ourselves, and each other. Grounded and gathered.

In another class, a first-year student from New York City described what it was like to come out of the subway station at Union Square and confront *Climate Clock* every day on her way to high school. Aware that the bright orange numbers, which display the time remaining to reduce carbon emissions and limit global warming to 1.5 degrees Celsius, increased her stress, she developed a protective strategy of emerging from the station and immediately averting her eyes. Her experience resonated closely with me and even surfaced some of my own emotions when I teach this vitally important work. And although the looming clock now includes a "lifeline" display (measuring the rising use of renewable sources of energy) along with its "deadline" display, it still seems to incite more fear than hope. Going forward, however, when feelings of eco-anxiety and climate grief take hold in and/or around me, I know just the thing. The walk in nature you quietly, softly led is an antidote. And now the practice you shared is in my tool kit, ready for use.

The nature walk was only one of the life-enhancing practices you shared that week. Two days later, Grace, Harrison, Willow, and Zola (the collaborators devoted to "Community, Compassion, and Conversation") asked us to pull our chairs into a tight circle. As I recall, Willow explained that she wanted us to experience a practice she knew well and knew to be true. It was a form of circle practice, and its intention was to build a common space where we could gather within a reflective and supportive community and share our stories and selves.[3] Of course, we

3
Educator Natalie Nikitas and students at Valor Collegiate Academies in Nashville discuss their circle practice as "a community of care," and share how the practice supports them in "building trust in a circle." "Brief but Spectacular," *PBS NewsHour*, February 19, 2024, https://youtu.be/hDXflBh8slo.

followed their good guidance. With empty hands and free of distractions, we sat shoulder to shoulder fearlessly sharing and tenderly listening to one another, person-to-person and face-to-face.

And how did it feel inside that circle?

Brave and caring. Slow and kind. Genuine and honest. And steeped in trust.

Which is to say, precisely how conversations should feel for everyone, everywhere.

What a powerful reminder it was of how community is created and sustained—what an essential practice of peace. And how lucky we were to try out both practices—the walk and the circle—in the very same week. One deepened our connections to the earth, while the other deepened our connections to each other.

It was in circle when Zola, a studio art and philosophy major, both shared her exceptionally generative thinking on "joyous activism" and bravely brought forward their anger, anguish, and profound sadness at the concerted cruelty of the forces fighting against justice, dignity, and peace.[4] Committed to a world where all belong and are free, they were experiencing despair given the cascading catastrophes. In tenderly listening to Zola's words, some of us, myself included, heard our own.

The late poet and activist June Jordan, driven by a fierce hope, reminds us that the true goal for our collective struggle for justice is to reach a place "where tenderness is possible."[5] By creating a practice space where together we could think, critically and creatively, along with socially engaged artists and art projects, we brought this future history closer into being.

In admiration and with a full and hopeful heart,
Lisa

Lisa Gail Collins
Professor of Art on the Sarah Gibson Blanding Chair and Director of the American Studies Program
Vassar College
Poughkeepsie, New York

4
Crucially, what is shared in a circle practice stays in the circle. I am grateful to Zola for their frank feedback on an earlier draft of this letter and for permission to share my recollection here.

5
June Jordan, in *A Place of Rage*, directed by Pratibha Parmer (Women Make Movies, 1991).

Story Line,
Art & Histories, Havana-Washington Island

Glexis Novoa

As literal as the journey of my life itself, this is the research that I performed to produce this piece. I discovered monuments and iconic locations in the cities of Havana and Washington, DC, with the intention of collecting an archive of images. This compendium of signs, packed with an intricate vocabulary, could well express the history of both nations, including notes on European colonizers and American liberators.

The same process led me to review a history saturated with dramatic events: wars, slavery, autocratic crises, blood and many deaths, perhaps too many martyrs. I revisited the experience of being a child indoctrinated in Marxism-Leninism, under the dogmatic word of an absolute leader and an Argentine commander. He was trying to create "The New Man" prior to the technology of deoxyribonucleic acid (DNA). All this made me recognize, very early on, the ideological programs hidden by the aesthetics of power—in the ideograms of the Chinese Cultural Revolution or the persistent runes of the cyrillic language of the Kremlin. As well, I participated in the political scenography spectacle, which covers the appearance of a city and all private spaces with centralized propaganda.

I learned how to live in a bubble, what today in the distance could be the past. Outside there was a real world, from which today I enter and leave, as the future. This leads me to have points of view from very peculiar perspectives—without iron curtains, without ever seeing the wall fall. The experience of exile became real, independent, and, at the same time, a vehicle to reread that forbidden history. That obsession, like a kind of nomadic doctrine of searching for horizons, collecting spaces, trying to dilute the panoramas and silhouettes of the cities, or decoding the discourse of the landscapes, has become the axis of my career. I have ended up telling stories using the encryptions that I have discovered along the way.

Art & Histories, Havana-Washington Island is a sort of compilation of enigmas, with which I can describe the intricate connection of these two nations, represented by the capitals of Havana and Washington, DC, that for so long have coexisted, almost dependent, against all possible odds. That is why I describe it as a unique panorama, represented on a large solitary island, where the monuments that speak of its history rest within a postapocalyptic metropolis. Perhaps inspired by the extensive solemnity of Arlington National Cemetery, the work is an exercise on the persistence of return, like the circular trip between a mother's and grandparents' houses.

Miami, 2024

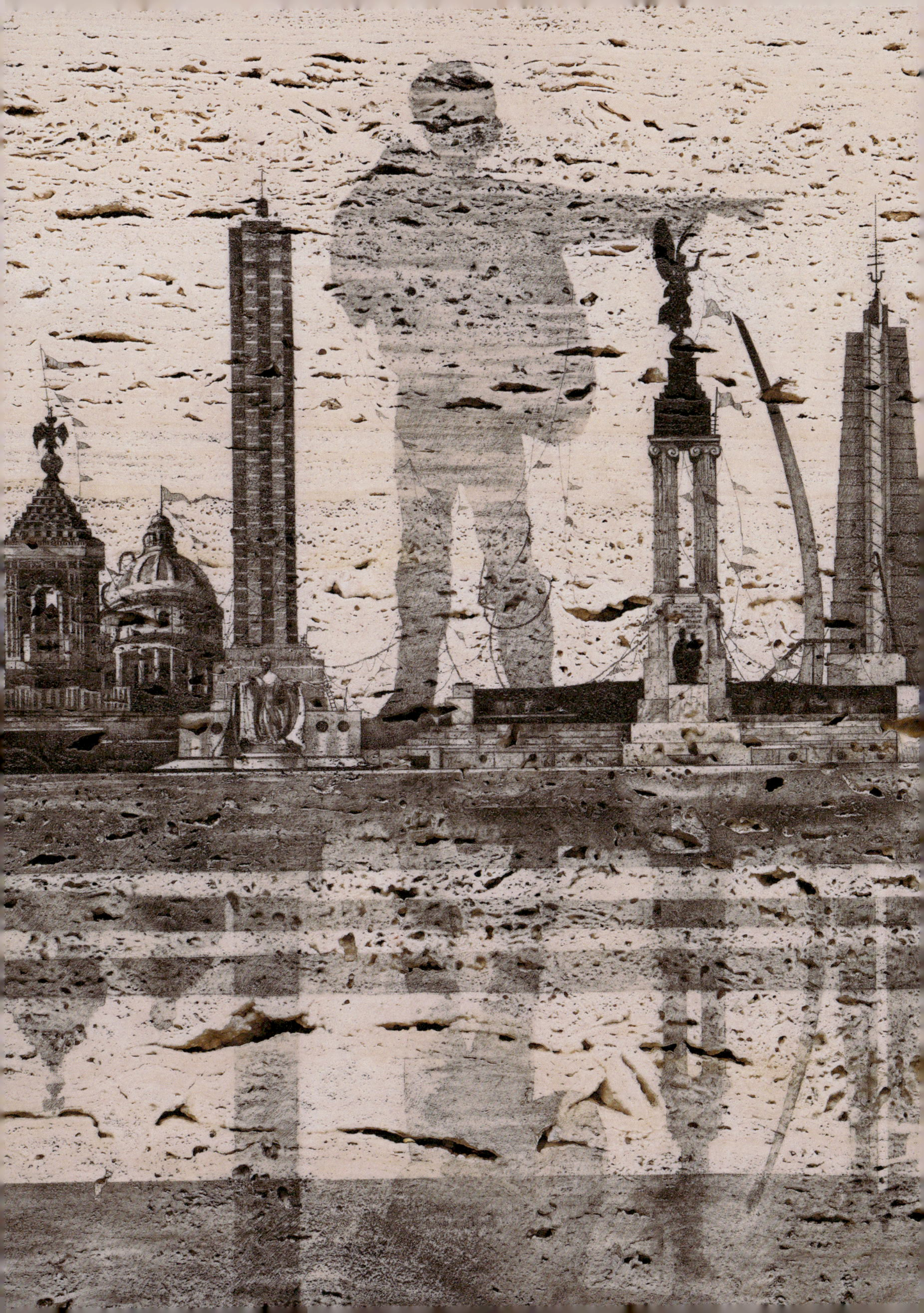

Glexis Novoa, *Art & Histories, Havana-Washington Island*, 2024, graphite on travertine marble, 45.7 × 121.9 cm

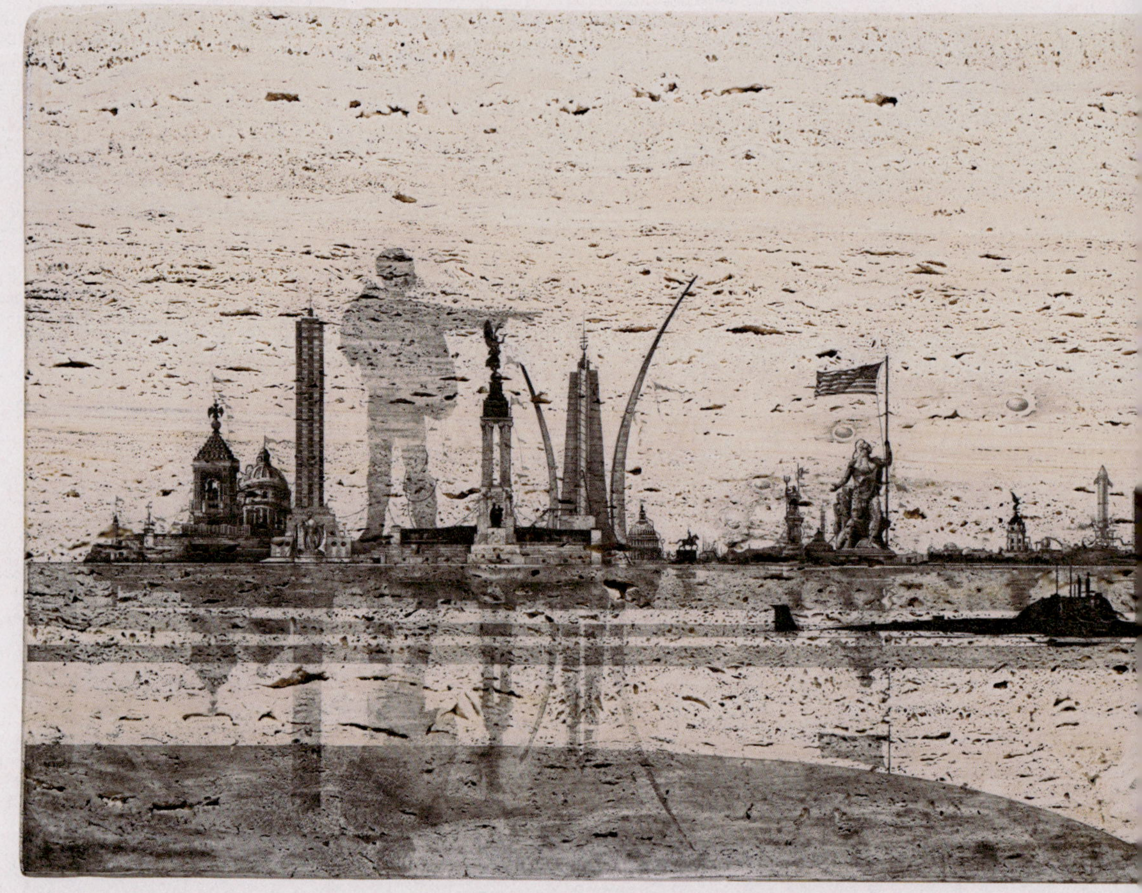

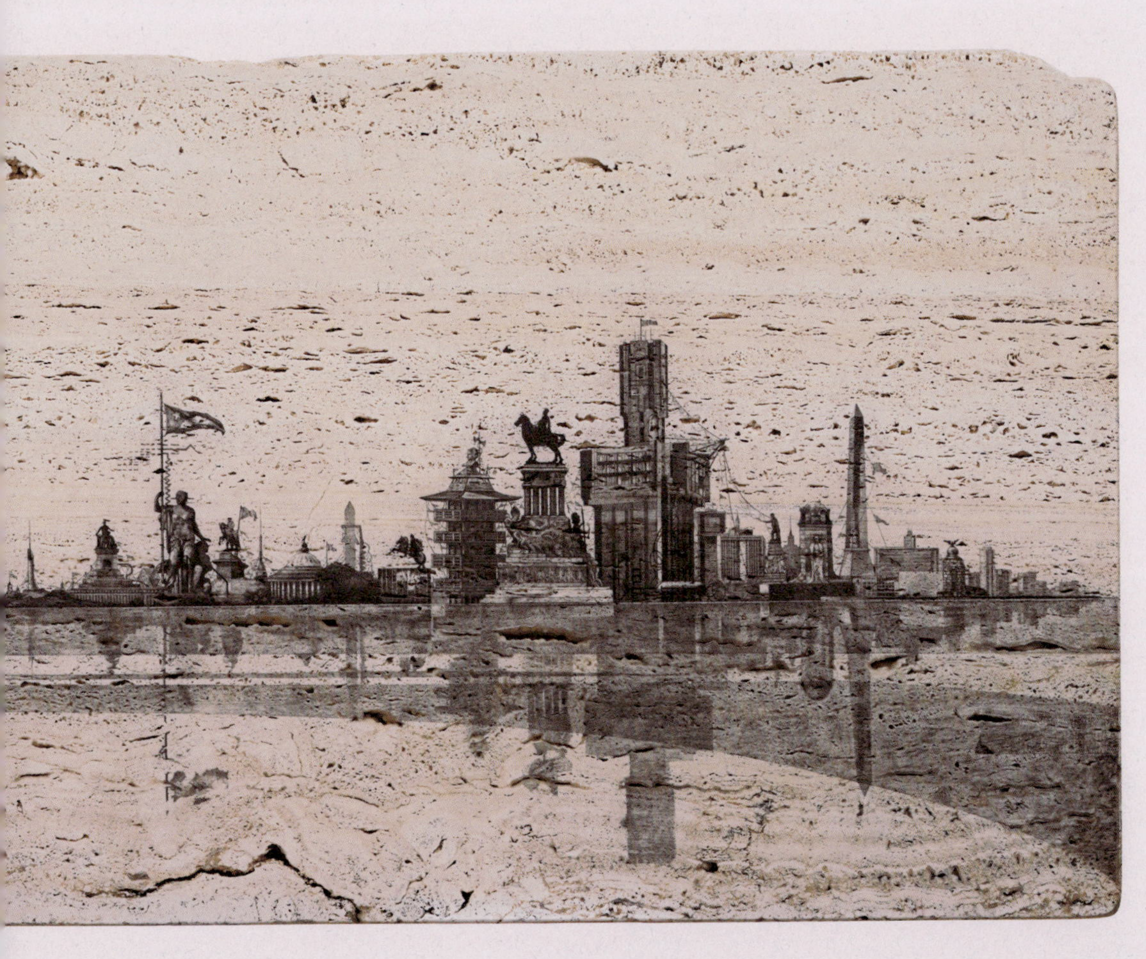

ESSAYS

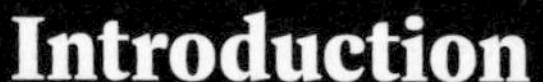

Introduction

Kaira M. Cabañas

The Art & series begins with "Histories," in its plural form, to signal an expansion of the study of art that embraces contemporary methods of art history and related disciplines. Though rooted in art's histories, each essay in this volume draws on and contributes to various methodologies and perspectives, including gender, Indigenous, performance, Black, and museum studies. Authors address subjects ranging from medieval dance and ancient Assyrian reliefs to expressions of gender embodiment and the art of the Afro-Atlantic. With an interdisciplinary framing grounded in expanded histories of art, *Art & Histories* foregrounds the material-aesthetic relations and theoretical affinities that motivate the essays' organization, while historicization of culturally specific concerns remains operative throughout.

Though the volume showcases "Histories" in its title, this first edition might well have been titled Art & Resistances or Art & Refusals, given the authors' shared ambition to practice *otherwise* the research and writing on art. Juno Richards questions our "unadulterated admiration" for the works of art to which we keep returning. Wanda Nanibush and, in a separate coauthored essay, Lorraine Mendes and Igor Simões confront the structural racism of the art system in the cultural contexts they engage (modern-day United States/Canada and Brazil, respectively). Seeta Chaganti charts how the art of pageantry is put into service policing bodies, minds, and property. Finally, Erhan Tamur argues against the perceived neutrality of museums. Just as each essay brings to mind the connections that exist in the visual arts among cultures that did not grow up separately from one another but were always already intertwined through colonial histories, cultural policies, and migrations, each author also actively embraces and illuminates further possibilities for scholarship and cultural responsiveness. From the seemingly modest request to address with honesty historical violence in museum wall labels (Tamur), to how an archive of dance can be mobilized for abolitionist horizons (Chaganti); from practicing a historiography that centers Black and Indigenous artists' contributions (Mendes and Simões; Nanibush), to reckoning *with* as a process by which to attend to, without resolving, historical injuries (Richards), these writers, rather than ask what art history *is*, task readers with productively imagining what art writing can *do* and to consider art's purchase on social worlds.

That one may turn to art's histories and pose them as a way of embodying possible futures is eloquently captured in the scenes of mutual learning that Lisa Gail Collins describes in an open letter to her students. She evokes how convening around the works and words of living artists creates a "generative space for reckoning with past and present histories and working to bring just and joyous future ones into being."[1] In this spirit of thinking *with* the works and words of living artists, Art & also features artist projects conceived and executed

1 Lisa Gail Collins, abstract submitted for *Art & Histories*, July 15, 2024.

specifically for the series. In this volume, Miami-based artist Glexis Novoa presents an accordion-fold insert with one of his signature horizon lines, uniting Washington, DC (the Center's home), and his native Havana. Meticulous drawings entangle the two cities and their monuments, symbolizing both violent and triumphant histories and their ideological reversals (i.e., one's loss is another's gain). Novoa's work juxtaposes imagined and real structures within a seemingly unified space informed by the tenets of Renaissance perspective and seventeenth-century Dutch landscapes.[2] His original drawings, executed on travertine marble, embody material specificity that necessarily contrasts with the presumed durability of monumental sculpture; the graphite drawings, more subject to the vicissitudes of time, eventually wear away.

From an editorial perspective, the aim of Art & has never been to provide a continuous genealogy or a comprehensive volume. Rather, in presenting a select constellation of essays, like the ones included in *Art & Histories*, the book casts in relief the singularity of its authors' voices and specific methodological approaches, which nevertheless share a common trait: Each reads past and present representations through past and present histories. Accordingly, the cumulative effect of reading the essays produces "new patterns of thinking-being," thereby reworking the contours of art's histories in ways that resonate with Karen Barad's dynamic approach to knowledge production, whereby the researcher and researched, subject and object, materiality and discursivity, remain entangled.[3] Rather than present reflections on past worlds, the authors' critical engagements, while committed to deep research and historical analysis, are also involved in the imagination and production of other worlds. I thus hope that, in reading and thinking with these authors, readers will come away with new insights about the arts and the evolving structures that determine how certain practices come to matter.

2 Kaira M. Cabañas, "In the beginning there was the Eye" (essay for Glexis Novoa's exhibition *Safe and Quiet*, Miami, fall 2002).

3 "Interview with Karen Barad," in *New Materialism: Interviews and Cartographies*, ed. Rick Dolphijn and Iris van der Tuin (Open Humanities Press, 2012), 58. See also my preface in the present volume.

Arts of Reckoning

Juno Richards

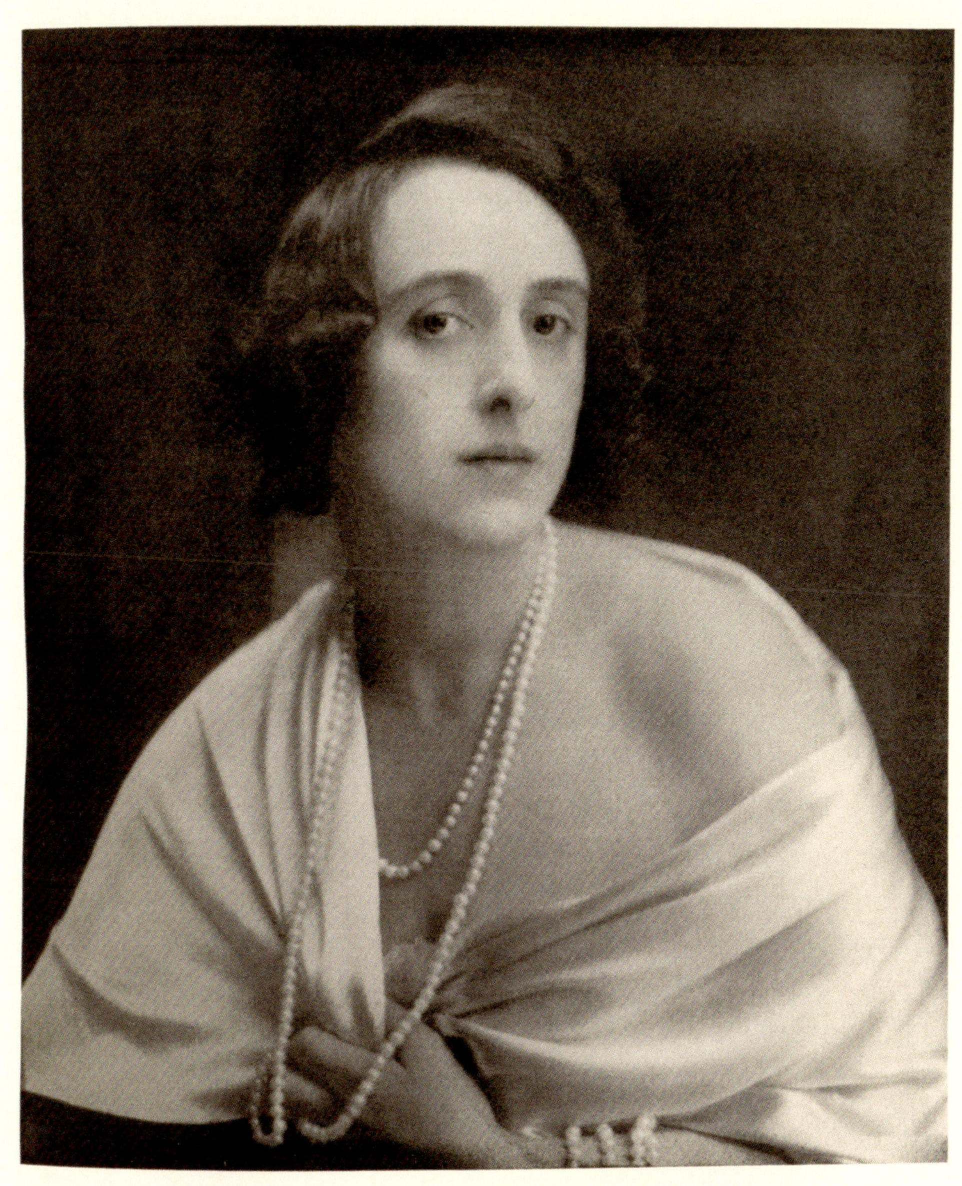

ORLANDO ON HER RETURN TO ENGLAND

The thing about getting older is that there is time to come back to a particular work of art again and again, to feel differently about it over the years. We are used to descriptions about the first encounter, the sudden infatuation or shock of recognition, as though that were the end of the story. But there is something to be said about living with the idea of a particular work, with its stories or figures, over time, as a matter of many returns. In the day-to-day, the year-to-year, the matter of coming back to the work, again and again, can infect the crevasses of a life.

It might be an ambivalent companionship. There is the matter of what leads you to return in the first place. There is the matter of what you might be hoping to find there. This is sometimes a story about disappointment and misplaced desire. On other days, it might look like a futile search for something that is not there. Some days the return could be a balm, a kind of aloe on the tongue. Others more like frustration, a circuit of agitation to solve an unsolvable puzzle.

But the fact of coming back, again and again, some years more than others, some years not at all, is itself a mode that needs to be reckoned with. Reckoning is here my preferred word, not repetition or return. In this case, the reckoning does not stem from unadulterated admiration. It comes out of the ways that the artwork is a political problem, and the ways that staying with it longer, thinking through

← Fig. 1 Lenare, "Orlando on Her Return to England," from *Orlando: A Biography* by Virginia Woolf (Hogarth Press, 1928), 145

the arc of its forms, accumulates. This accumulated time, what it means to return to an artwork, to spend time with it, is not itself a form of remedy or repair.

The work that has lived in the crevasses of my life is *Orlando*, Virginia Woolf's gender-bending fantasia, published in 1928. *Orlando* is a compounded, gemlike book, endlessly refractive and casually cruel. It's not a book that I love without condition. But I admire the way it unfolds in so many baroque and exquisite shapes, a too-muchness that is unapologetic in its sleights of hand, indefatigable with modifiers. This is style ratcheted up, guilelessly enthusiastic, as though saying *look, see this and this and this* that can be done with the nouns that name things—"a melon, a pineapple, an olive tree, and emerald, a fox in the snow."[1]

This writing is a lover's discourse, directed to a flesh and blood bisexual Vita Sackville-West, who also supplies the model for Orlando. Then Woolf's baroque style is not just exhibition for its own sake. It is a feat imagined as courtship, or more intimately a love letter, to the author's androgynous lover, who appears in a number of photographs inserted into the text (fig. 1). In taking up the imperial history of the Sackville estate, *Orlando* offers a history of landed wealth and the racial logistics of empire. Empire and this version of queer love are not just haphazard bedfellows. They are a part of each other's skeletal foundation.

1
Virginia Woolf, *Orlando: A Biography* (1928; Mariner, 1973), 28.

This intimacy, between empire and the love story of Orlando, appears on the first page, in the first sentence. The book begins with the decapitated head of a colonized person. Or rather, the first page begins with the matter of identifying Orlando's gender, then gets interrupted with an ongoing action, that of Orlando in the process of slicing the head off a mummied body:

> He—For there could be no doubt of his sex, though the fashion of the time did something to disguise it—was in the act of slicing the head of a Moor which swung from the rafters. It was the colour of an old football, and more or less the shape of one, save for the sunken cheeks and a strand or two of coarse, dry hair, like the hair on a cocoanut. Orlando's father, or perhaps his grandfather, had struck it from the shoulders of a vast Pagan who had started up under the moon in the barbarian fields of Africa; and now it swung, gently, perpetually, in the breeze which never ceased blowing through the attic rooms of the gigantic house of the lord who had slain him.[2]

The death is not a plot point for Woolf. The murder takes places offstage, somewhere else. The death is not mourned. The head itself is barely described, as object or plant matter. We do get a familial genealogy: It was not Orlando himself, but his aristocratic British ancestors who murdered this person during their plunder in Africa. The body hangs in the attic now as an anonymous trophy, a plaything for the aristocratic Orlando, just then a young man.

One explanation for this opening is satire. Woolf is revealing the histories of conquest that funded Britain's vast country estates, the very estates like Knole in which Orlando resides. The body hanging from the rafters is a way of making visible this legacy of racial violence. This is an adequate reading, but not one I particularly believe.

2
Woolf, *Orlando*, 11.

That first page cannot so easily be explained away. The explanation is an attempt to wrangle empire into a sentence or two, at the limits of what is forgivable.

I am starting from somewhere else, from a place that does not seek redemption. The first page is a horror made comic. The first page is a stain that grows worse the more you dab at it, each touch spreading the color out wrong. The first page is a hurt at the back of the throat that can't be swallowed down. Over years now of reading, I keep returning to the first page, frustrated, so that now the book just naturally bends there and stays open. It is grievous every time. I do not mean to say that the beginning is a key to the rest of the novel, which is sprawling and without a codex. *Orlando* is many things—a love letter, an epic of empire, a faux biography, a queer roman à clef, a feminist tour of the literary canon, and a science fiction of a five-hundred-year-old, ageless body who changes from male to female. The novel muddies genres and suggests new genres in turn to accommodate these accordion-like expansions of time and body.

It is the force of this invention, with its imagination of an infinitely flexible gendered body, that propels these compulsive returns, back to the first page, again. The rest of the book makes it worthwhile to try to understand the opening. But this understanding is no simple thing. The severed head on the first page of *Orlando* haunts the rest of the book. To come back to it, again and again, midway through, then near the end, then as a circle, back to front, is one way of making sense of this haunting.

This kind of reading turns *Orlando* into a series. To turn back to the first page from various midpoints changes the ways that narrative has a beginning and an end. Compulsive returns are one way of trying to get something right, to master an experience that ravaged you, as Woolf's contemporary Sigmund Freud famously argued.[3] But these returns to the first page are also a way of understanding relations between the center and its

3
See, for instance, Sigmund Freud, *Beyond the Pleasure Principle* (1920; Norton, 1990).

edges. To keep turning back to that first page is a way to imagine living through multiple genders alongside the history of empire, to hold these different things together in your hand. I would like to imagine each repelling the other, a tiny clawing and scratching under the fold of your knuckles. But it might be that, on some days, they are laid out into each other's clefts, settled together like spoons.

—

It is common, in this era, for trans autobiographies to picture gender indeterminacy as a quality made possible through the journey to a non-Western site. Drawing out the prevalence of travel across national borders in the wider arc of early Euro-American trans autobiographies, Aren Z. Aizura argues that normative transsexuality "becomes intelligible as a modern concept through its staging as a journey through 'elsewhere' spaces," including an orientalist East and a primitivist Africa.[4] In *Orlando* this possible "elsewhere" is Constantinople, where the young Orlando journeys as an agent of the British Empire. There, after a prodigious sleep, he wakes up in a woman's body, dresses herself in Turkish clothing, and leaves the imperial court to lead a nomadic life with the Romani people. To consider this episode according to a transgender and transnational analytic, as Jessica Berman does, allows the overt orientalism of the Turkish escapade to unfold doubly, as an imperial logic that contains a critique of empire within it, like the stone of a fruit or the meat of a walnut. Berman draws upon the ways that the male/female binary of gender can be traced to the eighteenth century, which also marks the rise of the nation-state. In Europe and the United States, this model of binary gender becomes part of the skeletal development of national civic identity, part of what constitutes "the very definition and policing of national identities."[5] However, in the Constantinople episode and after, the

4
Aren Z. Aizura, *Mobile Subjects: Transnational Imaginaries of Gender Reassignment* (Duke University Press, 2018), 4. For earlier work on the category of transgender in relation to border crossing, see Jack Halberstam, *In a Queer Time and Place: Transgender Bodies, Subcultural Lives* (NYU Press, 2005).

5
Jessica Berman, "Is the Trans in Transnational the Trans in Transgender?," *Modernism/modernity* 2, no. 2 (2017). For more on Orlando and transgender representation, see Jay Prosser, *Second Skins: The Bodily Narratives of Transsexuality* (Columbia University Press, 1998); Pamela L. Caughie, "The Temporality of Modernist Life Writing in the Era of Transsexualism: Virginia Woolf's *Orlando* and Einar Wegener's *Man into Woman*," *Modern Fiction Studies* 59, no. 3 (2013): 501–525.

→ Fig. 2 Vanessa Bell, Angelica Bell dressed as the Russian princess from Virginia Woolf's book titled *Orlando: A Biography*, taken at La Bergère in Cassis, near Marseille, 1928, black-and-white negative, 12.4 × 8.5 cm, Tate Archive, TGA 9020/11/20

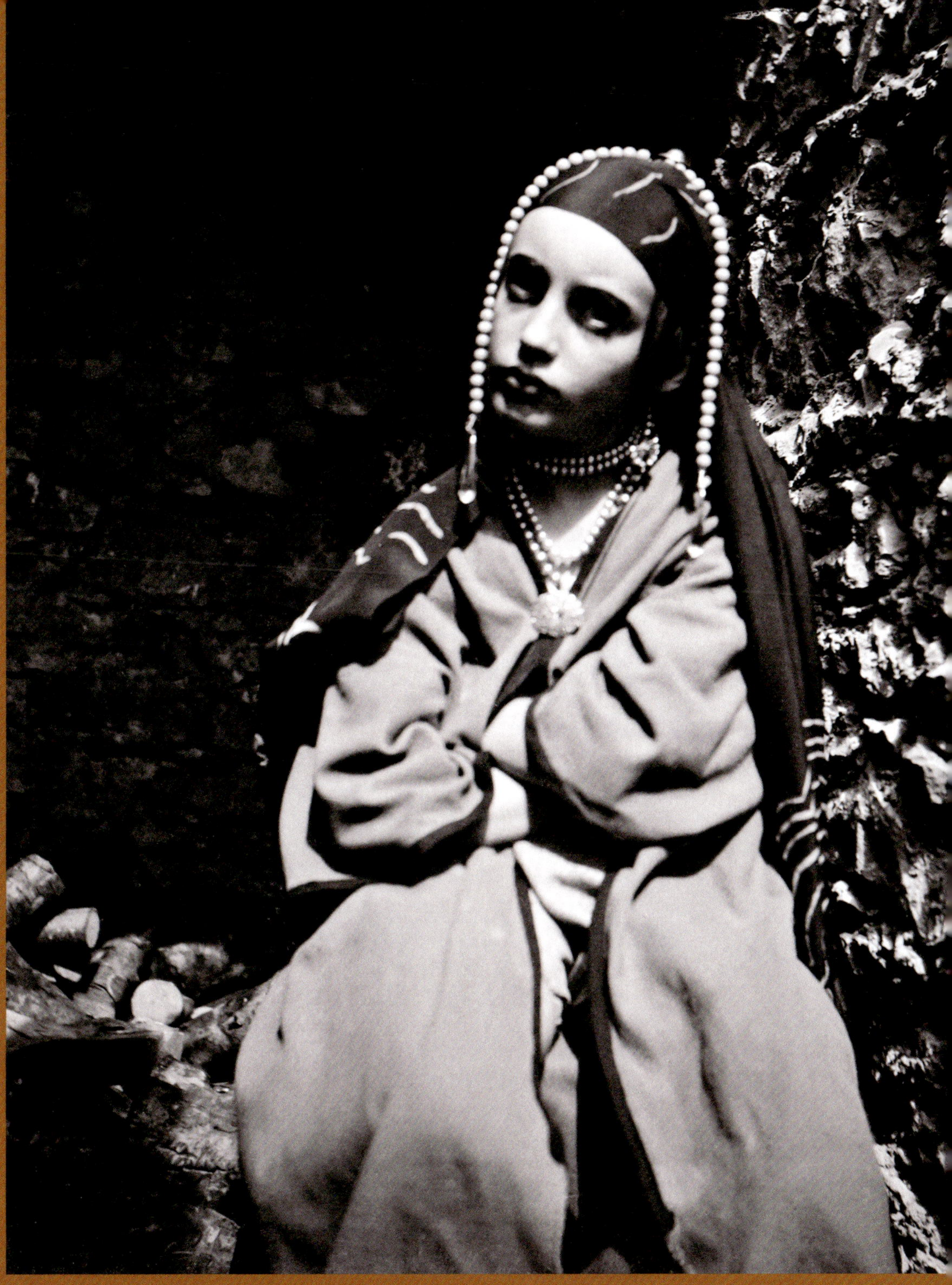

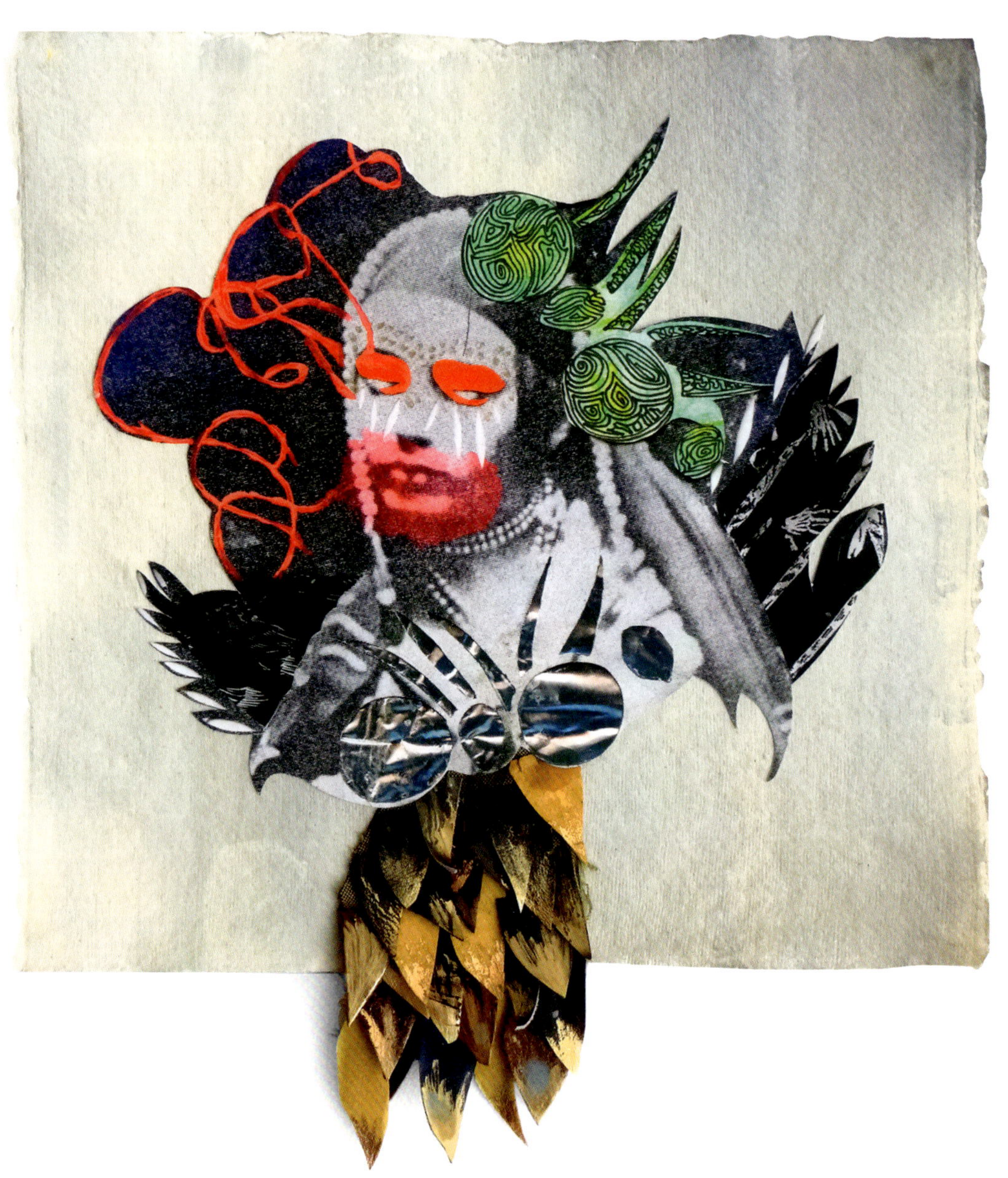

indeterminacy of Orlando's gender is an irritant to the binary logic that makes up legal forms of civic identity, one that challenges the ways that empire necessitates that the body "be identifiably marked, categorized, and placed in hierarchies" in order to be eligible for national inclusion.[6]

A repetition and a critique, a push back and a pull in. But one does not make up for the other. My initial formulation relied on metaphor—empire and its critique as the matter of a fruit and its stone, the meat of a walnut. These figures are misleading, because in each case one part gets left behind: the flesh of a plum eaten, the shell of the walnut cracked open. To reckon with the status of empire in *Orlando* means developing a different sort of language, one that can account for these modes as antagonists. This is a version of reckoning where we do not forget. The opening of the book remains in the frame of analysis, though it does not necessarily sit there alone.

—

In recent years, a number of visual and cinematic artists have made this reckoning their focus. These works return to *Orlando*, but they are not an homage. They are better understood as a grappling with the history of sexuality and empire, one that takes place through a play of identification and dis-identification.

Consider for instance Chitra Ganesh's multimedia collage *Catwoman Orlando*, which takes from the novel a rendering of the character Sasha, the Russian princess (figs. 2–3). Sasha is a puzzle for the young Orlando, in part because of her ambiguous gender, in part due to her ethnicity, racialized as a barbaric orientalism. This is pictured in the novel as an exotically savage nature, one that exceeds the metaphors and taxonomies of England.

6 Berman, "Is the Trans in Transnational."

← Fig. 3 Chitra Ganesh, *Catwoman Orlando*, c. 2013, collage of various papers, 30.5 × 35.6 cm

> [Sasha] was like a fox, or an olive tree; like the waves of the sea when you look down upon them from a height; like an emerald; like the sun on a green hill which is yet clouded—like nothing [Orlando] had seen or known in England. Ransack the language as he might, words failed him. He wanted another landscape, and another tongue. English was too frank, too candid, too honeyed a speech for Sasha.[7]

In the novel, the ostensible photograph of Sasha is in fact part of Woolf's personal archive, a picture of a costumed Angelica Bell, aged nine and photographed by her mother, Vanessa Bell, Woolf's sister. Ganesh's collage renders the already exotic child more creaturely, appending feathered wings to her shoulders and a kind of pelt from her breast. In Ganesh's hands, Sasha is part bird, part cat, with a foot and claws stamped onto her chest. The figure spills off the page with texture, at once a person and an animal, all claw and fang. In this way, *Catwoman Orlando* draws on the ways that Sasha is exiled from the boundaries of the human—as fox, stone, jewel, or landscape. But in Ganesh's hands, this rendering also turns the figure into a kind of weapon. The portrait is a surface that looks like it has been mauled a bit: the lines under the eyes, the unspooling of the red from their corners. It also looks like it might cut you were you to get too close to the razored edges.

In 2019 the photographer Mickalene Thomas restaged the portraits of *Orlando* as part of a series for a group exhibition centered around the novel and its filmic adaptation, directed by Sally Potter in 1992. Thomas recalls her encounter with the film when it first came out as a matter of recognition and desire both: "I wanted to be Orlando," she says. "As a teenager, when I was really coming to terms with my own sexuality, and was very much more androgynous than I am as my adult self, it felt so reassuring, safe, and exciting to see that on-screen."[8]

7
Woolf, *Orlando*, 34–35.

8
Mickalene Thomas, quoted in Antwaun Sargent, "Orlando Now," *Aperture*, July 3, 2019.

Thomas's photographs stage this mix of recognition and desire, but also hew to the discomfort of what it means to identify with a work that does not make space for your brand of subjectivity, at least not in the realm of the human. The photographs draw upon the Elizabethan section of the novel, playing upon early modern costumes. But the works mix these costumes with brightly colored backdrops and tropical flora, as though animating one of the jungled landscapes of Henri Rousseau.

In the studio portrait *Untitled #2* (*Orlando* series), Thomas restages the encounter between Queen Elizabeth and her squire Orlando, in what is itself a kind of autofiction. The queen is played by Racquel Chevremont, Thomas's longtime muse and partner, while the performance artist Zachary Tye Richardson stands in for Orlando (fig. 4). Like the other photographs in the *Orlando* series, this is a huge image, nearly four feet by five feet, all in jeweled colors set alongside intricate prints. But I want to draw out a tension here, a kind of agitation in the portrait between the staging of the sumptuously costumed aristocracy and the jungle backdrop, itself consisting of somewhat cheap-looking fake plants and Astroturf.

This photograph does double work. On one hand, it is a restaging of *Orlando* to center the racialized types relegated to the novel's orientalist margins. But this is not quite a triumph—the images are also haunted by the exoticism of Rousseau, here made cheap and rickety. The flimsiness of the jungle backdrop stresses the falseness of the cliché, rather than a kind of truth.

We can see a similar gesture in the recent feature film *Orlando, My Political Biography*, written and directed by Paul B. Preciado, the Spanish-born activist and philosopher. In this work, his feature directorial debut, Preciado renders *Orlando* as a collective biography—there is not one *Orlando*, but many. Each actor enters with an introduction, one that places a chosen name and the fact of performance: "I'm Janis Sahraoui. In this film I'll be

Fig. 4 Mickalene Thomas, *Untitled #2*, *Orlando* series, c. 2019, chromogenic dye coupler print, 109.9 × 146.7 cm

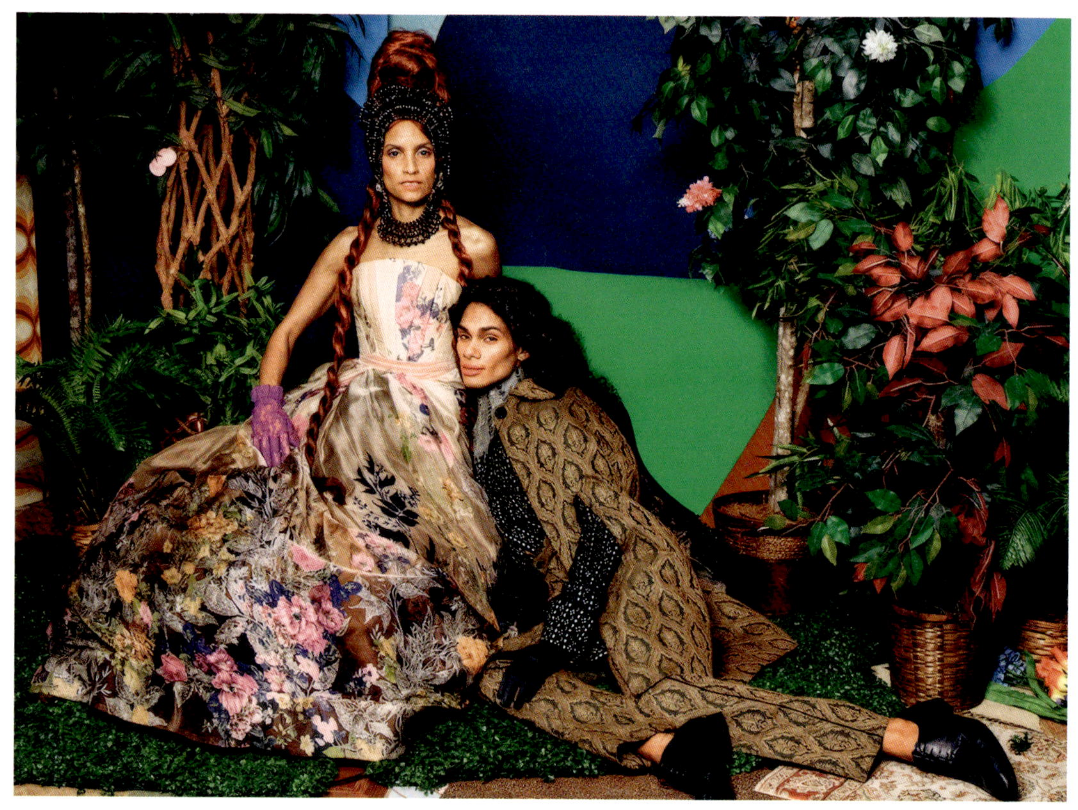

Fig. 5 Film still from *Orlando, My Political Biography*, directed by Paul B. Preciado, 2023

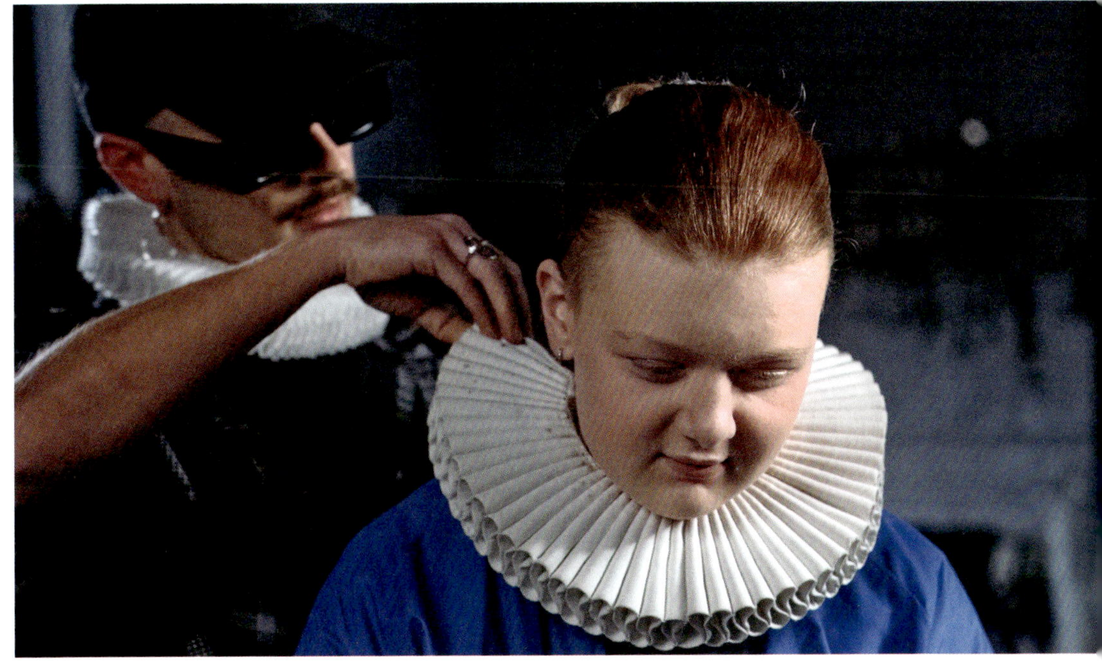

Orlando by Virginia Woolf." "My name is Oscar Rosza Miller. In this film I'll be Orlando by Virginia Woolf." "I'm Jenny Bel'Air. And in this film I'll be Orlando by Virginia Woolf." "I am Koriangelis Brawns. And in this film I'll be Orlando by Virginia Woolf."[9] No one gets to be Orlando precisely; instead there are many Orlandos. Elders, teens, trans women, and children try on Orlando as a version of personhood that doesn't quite fit, a strangeness made visible by the Elizabethan collar sported by many of the actors and the Boston terrier that prances through much of the film (fig. 5).

In one such scene, four Orlandos wear their lace collars with surgical masks and scrubs in order to perform surgery on a hardback first edition of *Orlando*. The book is wheeled into the darkened surgical suite on a hospital bed, then transferred to the operating table. The Orlandos set their scalpels to the text, slicing out photographs of Vita Sackville-West and her ancestors, placing them in a receptacle with forceps, then laying in new photographs, neatly sewn into the page with surgical wire. They cut out the portrait of the Honorable Edward Sackville, son of the 4th Earl of Dorset, and transfer into his place a photograph of trans icons Marsha P. Johnson and Sylvia Rivera. Preciado includes a photograph of himself as "a nonbinary, five-year-old Orlando," glowering at the camera in a pink suit.[10]

From some angles, the surgical interlude verges on blithe optimism. Would that all that were necessary were some cutting and pasting, sewing in one photograph for another, to address historical wrongs. It is possible to chafe at this humor or regard it as naive. But such irritation misses the film's flagrant absurdity. The surgical tableau is an elaborate satire, one that replaces the materiality of the flesh—and the very real matter of access to gender-affirming surgery—with a solution that is patently ridiculous. This is a picturing of historical repair as absurdist comedy, a dark humor indeed. It is a reckoning with the colonial legacy of *Orlando* that offers a slant

9
Orlando, My Political Biography, directed by Paul Preciado (Janus Films, 2023).

10
Preciado, *Orlando, My Political Biography*.

way of making claims. In this rendering, two narratives coexist: the desire for a reckoning with the past and the acknowledgment that historical injury cannot be so easily made good through better representation—merely a matter of different photographs, sewn into the record with wire.

To call *Orlando, My Political Biography* a reckoning illuminates both meanings of the word. There is a calculation here, a sizing up, alongside an encounter with past mistakes. As Preciado puts it, "Someone once asked me, why don't you write your biography? I replied, because fucking Virginia Woolf wrote my biography in 1928. I'm sorry I said fucking Virginia Woolf. I said it with tenderness and admiration because your writing seemed impossible to surpass. But also I say it with rage because you represented us trans people as aristocrats in colonial England."[11]

An admixture of tenderness, admiration, and rage then: Across this suite of serial returns, Ganesh, Thomas, and Preciado all retain some element of the original text alongside its revision. In these renderings, the serial return is not a solution. To return to a work again and again, over time, to spend time with its stories, to live in or as it, does not necessarily result in repair. All that time does not necessarily make good on historical injury. The reckoning with *Orlando* is instead a matter of agitation between modes. There is the misfit past and its reconstructed present, not as a scene of repair, concluded, but something in motion, visibly constructed out of opposites. It is a reckoning with *Orlando* that leaves the wire stitches showing on the cutout page, the landscape Astroturf and other flimsy plastic plants just on the verge of tipping over.

11
Preciado, *Orlando, My Political Biography*.

This Performer Is Not an Artifact

Wanda Nanibush

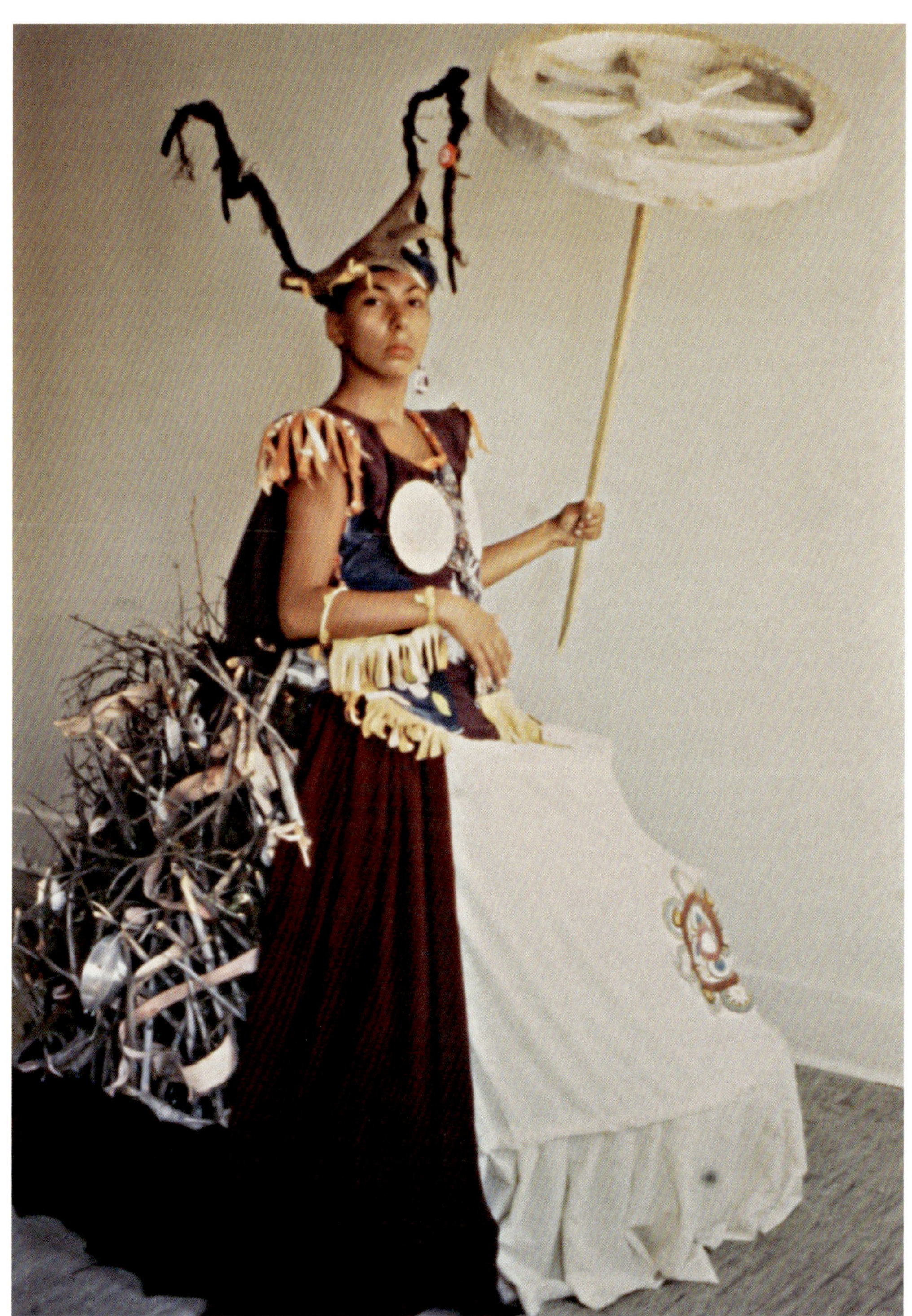

It is my feeling that artwork in the medias of Performance and Installation offers an opportunity like no other for Indian people to express themselves in traditional art forms of ceremony, dance, oral traditions and contemporary thought, without compromise.
—James Luna[1]

It had a lot to do with the climate of art at that moment, where it made sense to me to be the art, to be the performance artist—to wear the work, to be inside the work, to exhibit the work....I thought to be within my own skin was the most authentic thing that I could do, from my perspective as an Indigenous woman.
—Rebecca Belmore[2]

In this essay, I take 1987 as a moment to examine a monumental shift in the place of Indigenous art within a contemporary discourse in the United States and Canada.[3] More precisely, I turn to James Luna's *The Artifact Piece* (1987) at the San Diego Museum of Man and, a year later, Rebecca Belmore's performance *Artifact #671B* (1988) outside the Thunder Bay Art Gallery. These well-known works by performance artists mark the entry of Indigenous artists into contemporary art, clearing the ground of Indigenous representations that hold artists back

← Rebecca Belmore (Anishinaabe), *Rising to the Occasion*, 1987, performed at Definitely Superior Art Gallery, Thunder Bay

from being properly considered "contemporary." Performance art, which defines itself against other art forms found to be more amenable to commodification and aesthetic classification, was an important choice for these artists in order to embody a power shift from capital-H History as reenactment and reification of colonial power to embodied histories that bring to life Indigenous ways of seeing and being. Not only did these works and subsequent performances through 1992 bring about new art historical trajectories, but they also paved the way for new models of Indigenous art.

—

Before turning to the specific works, I offer here an extremely quick sketch of North American Indigenous politics in the 1980s. This is necessary to understand what artists were living through and what a larger political project of self-determination might mean from an Indigenous perspective. The eighties were decisively a politically conservative time with Brian Mulroney in Canada, Ronald Reagan in the United States, and Margaret Thatcher in Britain. It was a time of continued constitutional and legal discussions and decisions on Indigenous rights. The repatriation of the Canadian Constitution Act of 1982 brought about massive protests as well as petitions to Queen Elizabeth II to honor treaties. Treaties are nation-to-nation agreements between individual First Nations governments and the British Crown. Indigenous folks argued that their treaties were with the Crown and that Canada had no legal standing to abrogate First Nations' sovereignty. Canada's response was to enshrine Aboriginal and treaty rights into the 1982 Constitution Act under Section 35: "The existing aboriginal and treaty rights of the aboriginal peoples of Canada are hereby recognized and affirmed."

A series of First Ministers' conferences (FMC) from 1983 to 1987 were held with Indigenous leaders to decide the meaning of "existing" rights. According to legal scholar Douglas Sanders, "the aboriginal organisations had formed a solid coalition and insisted on the recognition of an inherent right of self-government. The right must be 'free standing', that is a clear, unqualified, non-contingent statement of a right of self-government. There should be additional provisions establishing a negotiating process to define the powers of self-government."[4] The Canadian government rejected this idea and instead Mulroney put forward a draft that read: "The aboriginal peoples of Canada have the right to self-government within the context of the Canadian federation."[5] This rewriting was rejected by all the Aboriginal organizations because it meant that their sovereignty was not inherent as First Peoples but instead derived from Canada's sovereignty. Sanders rightfully acknowledged that though the FMC process failed, "the treaty process has never been ended in Canada. It is a bilateral process, between First Nations and Canada. Past present and future treaties are constitutionally recognised by section 35(1). This process is available if the First Nations and Canada agree to use it."[6]

Whereas the FMC proved unsuccessful in Canada, the 1980s brought about a few notable court cases in the United States, wherein Native Americans asserted their inherent rights to hunt, fish, and regulate their economies. One standout court ruling is the Voigt decision (1983)

1
James Luna, "Allow Me to Introduce Myself," *Canadian Theatre Review* 68 (Fall 1991): 46.

2
Rebecca Belmore, quoted in Wanda Nanibush, "Rebecca Belmore: All of My Relations," *Aperture*, Fall 2020.

3
As a beginning, it's helpful to map the language shifts in how we have been named. We no longer use the word Indian because it is a misnomer that erases our subjectivity, nationhood, and diversity, as well as being tied to racist legislation, the Indian Act of 1876. The one exception is for those of us who use it among ourselves to describe the experience of assimilation policies, reservation life, racism, and the solidarity that comes when you meet others who have been through it too. Native became popular in the 1960s, and to a large extent still is. It had to be capitalized to distinguish First Peoples from any native who is born in a place. Peoples was added to Native to account for the diversity of nations the word contained. Aboriginal Peoples refers to section 35 of the 1982 Canadian Constitution Act, which states that "aboriginal and treaty rights are hereby recognized and affirmed." Aboriginal Peoples includes First Nations, Inuit, and Métis. Aboriginal is not widely liked due to the meaning of "Ab" (not), which then means "not original." It's also a word imposed and not chosen, like Indian. First Nations became a word that marked both our nationhood and firstness on this land now called Canada. Eventually it was used for specific reservation-bounded bands, which meant it could no longer be used for all First Peoples, including Inuit and Métis. I still use it for all First Peoples. First Nations is also starting to become common in the United States and Australia. In the United States, Native American has become common. Indigenous has been used since the 1970s for international First Peoples. Indigenous also cites the United Nations Declaration on the Rights of Indigenous Peoples and implies global connections and rights. Some people like Indigenous because it speaks to a connection to the land. Indigenous comes from the Latin word *indigena*, which means "sprung from the land; native." Some First Nations in Australia do not like the name Indigenous because it's too close to being labeled flora and fauna, which was how they were categorized under the law there. We only have to come up with general all-encompassing terms for the convenience of colonialism, which has lumped us all together as one when for millennia we were many nations with our own governance systems, beliefs, medicines, philosophies, sciences, education systems, and social structures, with territories and ways of being. In general, each nation prefers its own name for itself in its own language.

4
Douglas Sanders, "Canada: The First Minister's Conferences on Aboriginal Rights," *Aboriginal Law Bulletin* 8 (1987).

5
Sanders, "Canada."

6
Sanders, "Canada."

in which the Anishinaabe (Ojibwe) in Wisconsin were deemed free from state regulations within their reservation boundaries, and thus continued to spear hunt. The backlash turned into the so-called Walleye War led by Stop Treaty Rights Abuse and Protect America's Rights and Resources. To combat this anti-Indigenous sentiment, Wisconsin Act 31 (1989) mandated "instruction in the history, culture and tribal sovereignty of the federally recognized American Indian tribes and bands located in this state at least twice in the elementary grades and at least once in the high school grades."[7] The hope was that by educating students about treaty obligations, a more aware population would be created—one that would stop fighting Indigenous rights.

Subsequently, the 1987 *Cabazon v. California Band of Mission Indians* case was decided in the US Supreme Court, which upheld Native American sovereignty over their economies and lands. This decision gave birth to casinos all over Native America through the Indian Gaming Regulatory Act of 1988. Much like the Canadian government, the Reagan administration supported sovereignty only in terms of small, municipal-style governments that it hoped would save the federal government money.[8] In 1987, on the occasion of the bicentennial of the US Constitution, Reagan inaugurated Native American ~~Indian~~ Week in order to recognize that "the Constitution affirmed the special relationship of the Federal government with American Indians when it stipulated, 'the Congress shall have Power To... regulate commerce with foreign Nations, and among the several States, and with the Indian Tribes...' This unique government-to-government relationship continues today and has been reinforced through treaties, laws, and court decisions."[9]

From Canada's Section 35 to the United States' Native American ~~Indian~~ Week, this overview shows how our political and physical existence is decided in a colonial context by governments, courts, and legislators who

7
See Eric Jurgens, review of *The Story of Act 31: How Native History Came to Wisconsin Classrooms*, by J.P. Leary, *Journal of American Indian Higher Education* 30, no. 3 (Spring 2019).

8
"Statement on Indian Policy," January 24, 1983, Reagan Library Archives; Adrienne M. Davidson, "Incomplete Sovereigns: Unpacking Patterns of Indigenous Self-Governance in the United States and Canada," *American Review of Canadian Studies* 49, no. 2 (2019): 262–282.

9
"Proclamation 5745—American Indian Week, 1987," November 19, 1987, Reagan Library Archives.

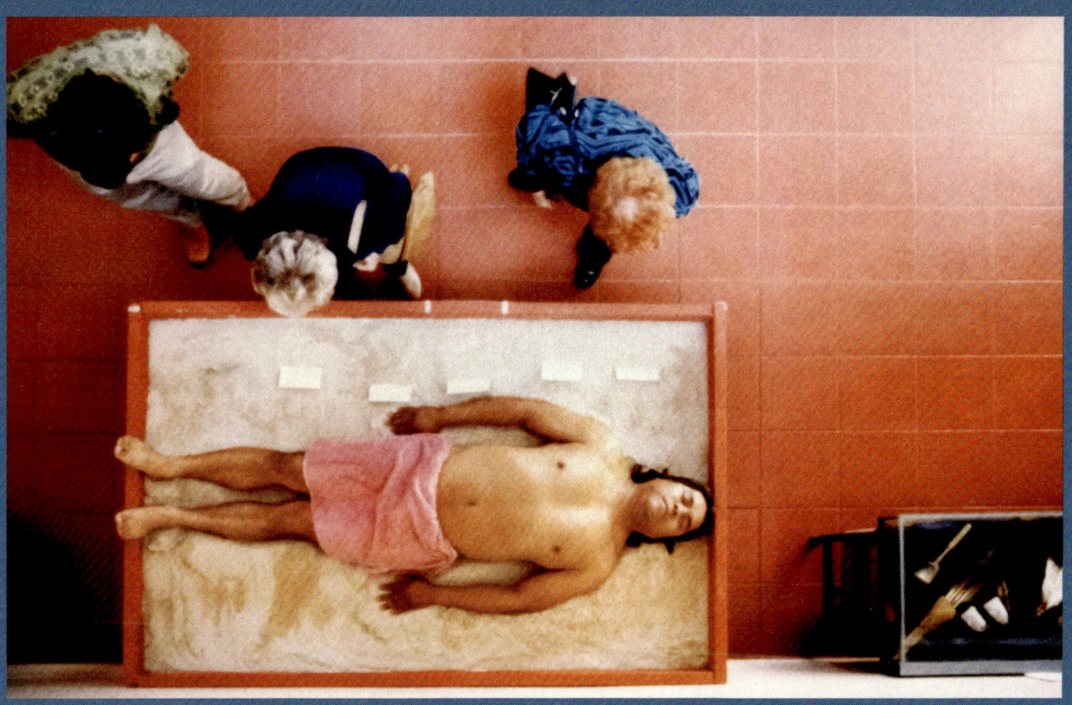

Fig. 1 James Luna (Payómkawichum and Mexican American), *The Artifact Piece*, 1987, performed at San Diego Museum of Man

are not Indigenous. We resist, ignore, fight, and assert our rights constantly. This is also true of representation within the arts, which is directly and indirectly tied to political action and aspiration. Representation has very real material effects, which underscore the importance of Indigenous artists critiquing representations and building their own in order to bring about spaces of cultural, political, and physical freedom. Nowhere is this clearer than in the work of James Luna and Rebecca Belmore. While Luna starts with writing, carefully planning his actions and scripting his words (often using props, video, and photography), Belmore starts from a site or an event, and then builds a visual language and set of actions that are roughly planned but respond to the moment. Both have an incredible sense of irony and are unafraid to place their body on the line in contemporary debates on the state and status of First Nations people. In choosing performance art as a starting point for their installation work, they break with the temporary and physical segregation of Indigenous peoples that keeps their contemporaneity under erasure.

—

In 1987, when he was director of education for the La Jolla Indian Reservation, James Luna was invited to organize an exhibition at the San Diego Museum of Man, an institution that was formed as part of the civilizing and assimilation discourses of world's fairs. Industrial breakthroughs were often exhibited alongside living Indigenous peoples from all over the world, contrasting the civilized with a primitiveness that became the dominant view of Indigenous cultures: authentic only in the precontact past, savage, and left behind or ruined by modernity. Museums became a place to display the often ill-gotten goods of precontact Indigenous cultures, thereby casting them as purely past, ahistoric, and unchanging. The reality of modernizing Indigenous people was not valued, or seen as contaminated and ignoble. The desire was to preserve Indigenous knowledge, but not necessarily Indigenous peoples. Our disappearance was considered inevitable though our knowledge had a use value for the future of the "new" nations (Canada and the Unites States).

Luna, a Payómkawichum and Mexican American artist, decided to respond to this institutional and discursive context by performing as an artifact in the museum (fig. 1).[10] Performance art as a practice often deals with the history of a site and its interaction with the artist through their physical embodiment. In *The Artifact Piece*, Luna was placed inside a case at the San Diego Museum of Man, lying down on sand and dressed in a loincloth. The museum label pointed out different scars on his body and their origin stories. Another vitrine housed his favorite music, family photos, divorce papers, a college degree, and other personal artifacts. For the visitor, it became clear that Luna was a living, breathing, contemporary artist who enjoyed music, had endured hard times, and loved his community and family. For the work, Luna had to remain still for hours a day with shallow breathing. He said he prayed to the Creator, looking for strength, before he was laid in the case. By performing in this way, Luna defied the museum's Native collections, demonstrating his acute awareness of how the display of Indigenous cultures is part of what keeps contemporary Indigenous peoples unthinkable.

Luna, however, was unprepared for how angry he felt listening to visitors talk about him when he couldn't respond. He describes his experience with the first visitor:

> I heard the steps, coming up the steps and the chatter
> Looking at the artifacts of the various PEOPLES of the world
> Mostly tribal

10 Luna was born in 1950 in Orange, California, and moved to the La Jolla Indian Reservation in 1975. He passed away in 2018 from a heart attack while attending an artist residency at the Joan Mitchell Center in New Orleans.

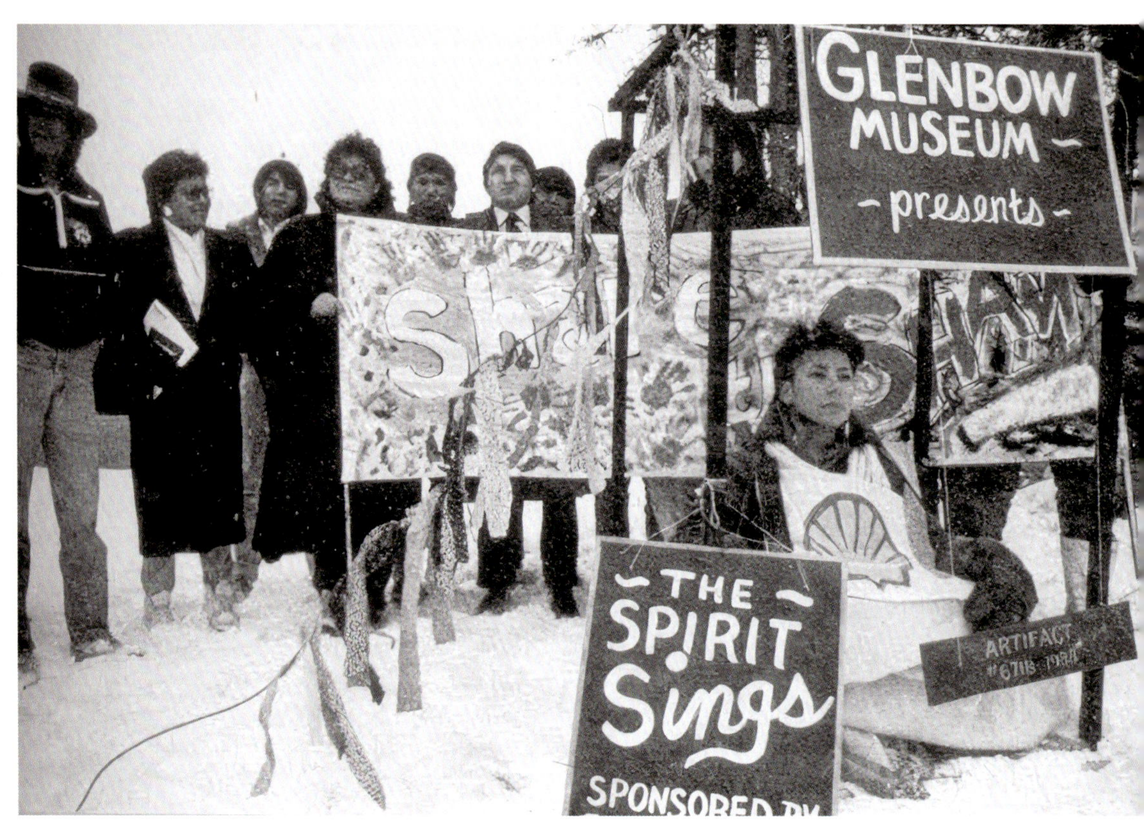

Fig. 2 Rebecca Belmore (Anishinaabe), *Artifact #671B*, 1988, performed outside Thunder Bay Art Gallery

All about the past
All about the past
As though we don't exist in the present
Until they saw me
So I filtered out the sounds
Though I could still hear them
And the first voice I heard was
"Hey this guy's alive"
(Sounds of confusion and awe)
Wow wow
They paying him for this[11]

Luna's use of his subjective lived experience as a particular Native American who faced colonialism's effects was a deep counter to the salvage ethnography within the San Diego Museum of Man and the broader culture.[12] In an interview published in *Smithsonian Magazine*, Luna revealed that the inspiration for his work was a critique of anthropological museums: "I had long looked at representation of our peoples in museums and they all dwelled in the past. They were one-sided. We were simply objects among bones, bones among objects, and then signed and sealed with a date. In that framework you really couldn't talk about joy, intelligence, humor, or anything that I know makes up our people."[13] What was lost in the construction of the "authentic" Indian was Indigenous peoples' subjectivity and their inherent capacity to represent themselves, as well as the processes of violence that make such artifacts available for salvage.

Constant in all discursive constructions of the "noble savage" or the alterity of Indigenous peoples is a systematic appropriation of their cultures, bodies, and territories as objects of study. Ronald W. Hawker argues that "since colonized societies and the objects they produced were necessarily destroyed by the process of colonization, it was the duty of those at the forefront of modernity's intrusion into the societies of the 'less advanced' to vigorously record what colonialism displaced."[14] Modern nostalgia for the past was monitored

11 "Real Faces: James Luna: La Nostalgia: The Artifact," posted December 7, 2009, by deCoy Gallerina, YouTube, https://www.youtube.com/watch?v=iLKRohvCMx0.

12 On salvage ethnography, see Johannes Fabian, *Time and the Other: How Anthropology Makes Its Object* (Columbia University Press, 1983).

13 Kenneth R. Fletcher, "James Luna," *Smithsonian Magazine*, April 2008.

14 Ronald W. Hawker, *Tales of Ghosts: First Nations Art in British Columbia, 1922–61* (University of Chicago Press, 2003), 26.

and released by constructing a record of the colonial "other" and the "facts" of its cultures. Luna turns this discourse against itself by presenting a beautifully flawed and ultimately living embodiment of the effects of modernity. By becoming the exhibit, he effectively shocks viewers out of their complacent acceptance of the museum narrative, hoping to impact their view of Indigenous artists and the politics of sovereignty.

The art world Luna worked in had absorbed the "authenticity" discourse to the point where Native art was only *seen* as such if it "looked" Native—meaning that artists needed to leverage signs of "Indianness" in their work (e.g., breechclout-wearing horseback riders, feathers, beads, leather, Plains Natives or Pueblo scenes) to be recognizable by a non-Native audience. This oppressive edict that art had to look "Native" made it difficult for individuals to be taken seriously as contemporary artists. In being marked as outside time or in the past, Indigenous artistic production was only seen as modern at the moment when "the West" was already postmodern, in the 1980s, whereby Native art was evaluated as derivative of the West, as a poor copy, or as traditional and thus craft.

Margaret Dubin captures this phenomenon, also drawing attention to the year 1987, through a story of a Native American artist who carved sculptures. A gallerist in Sedona told the artist, "Sorry. They're just not Indian enough."[15] Such a judgment tethers a negative market value to increased artistic experimentation. It follows that an Indigenous artist wanting to make a living from sales would need their work to "look Indian," thus discouraging freedom of expression. This constraint, one defined by commercial expectations based in a racial and colonial imaginary, has also impacted other artists of color, including Black and Latinx artists in the United States. Luna felt the repercussions of this: "somewhere in the mass, many Indian artists forgot who they were by doing work that had nothing to do with their tribe, by

15
Margaret Dubin, *Native America Collected: The Culture of an Art World* (University of New Mexico Press, 2001), 1.

16
Luna, "Allow Me to Introduce Myself," 46–47.

doing work that did not tell about their existence in the world today, and by doing work for others and not for themselves."[16] With *The Artifact Piece*, Luna cleared the ground with his own body to create space for Native cultures within the contemporary art scene, displacing colonial divisions of precontact purity and (post)colonial contamination; authentic and ignoble; civilized and primitive.

—

Up north in Thunder Bay, across the US-Canada border that divides Native peoples without their permission, a young Anishinaabe performance artist was creating work outside of the city center. Only a few months after Luna, on a winter day outside of the Thunder Bay Art Gallery, Rebecca Belmore put herself in a vitrine as *Artifact #671B* (fig. 2). The two artists did not yet know each other, and yet in making similar work, they arguably showed the necessity of first contending with white expectations of authentic Indigenous cultures before creating space for themselves as contemporary artists. Belmore sat cross-legged in her vitrine, with the Shell Oil logo on her coat and signs reading "Glenbow Museum presents" and "Spirit Sings sponsored by Shell Oil." Using performance art's capacity to respond to contemporary events, she embodied the underlying rage at the use of historical artifacts to undermine Indigenous sovereignty.

More specifically, Belmore wanted to bring attention to the Lubicon Cree First Nations' boycott of the exhibition *The Spirit Sings: Artistic Traditions of Canada's First Peoples*, which showcased historical belongings of Indigenous peoples and was organized by the Glenbow Museum in Calgary as part of their participation in the 1988 Winter Olympics Arts Festival. The exhibition and the Olympics were sponsored by Shell Oil, which at the same time was drilling on Lubicon land with the support of the Albertan government. The call for a boycott was an assertion of Lubicon sovereignty as they tried to protect their hunting lands and way of life. They had never ceded their lands to the Crown in a treaty and thus held inherent title, which was supposed to be protected by Section 35 of the 1982 Constitution Act. Belmore understood the relationship between *The Spirit Sings* and sovereignty. As long as we were presented as relics of the past through our belongings held in museums, contemporary land claims or cultures could not be understood as legitimate. Sovereignty becomes a headache to soothe in court cases, legislation, and museums. Belmore used her living body, holding her pose for hours in weather of negative eighteen degrees Celsius.

—

Luna and Belmore each challenged representational erasure and affirmed the power of a gesture of defiance. Belmore heard about Luna's performance and applied to do a residency with him later that year, in 1988. The two immediately found a colleague and a friend in each other. Their work was different and there was a decade between them, but both are considered to be the artists that kicked open the doors to an embodied practice that challenged the borders of a contemporary art scene that excluded First Nations artists.

While museums relegated Indigenous "authenticity" to the past, art education also taught the artists how others would attempt to legislate their practices on account of their identities. Luna and Belmore began art school studying the more traditional pursuits of painting and sculpture before turning to performance art after experiences with racism. Belmore said that one of her professors at Ontario College of Art in Toronto asked her, in her second year-end critique, "if I thought my 'Indian-ness' would get in the way of making art. It made me speechless and then angry…I decided I should go home and make art. Become one, an Artist."[17] For Luna, he thought the art degree "was gonna expand my

17
Rebecca Belmore, quoted in Wanda Nanibush, "An Interview with Rebecca Belmore," *Decolonization: Indigeneity, Education & Society* 3, no. 1 (2014): 213.

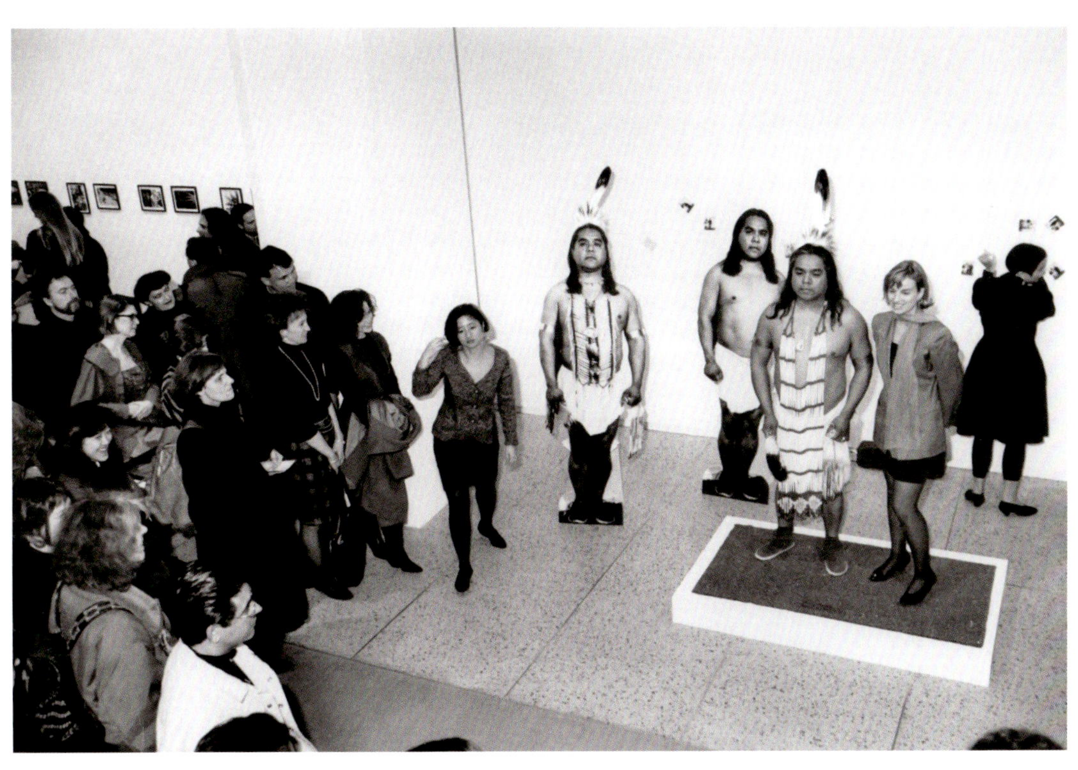

Fig. 3 James Luna (Payómkawichum and Mexican American), *Take a Picture with a Real Indian*, 1991, performed at Whitney Museum of American Art

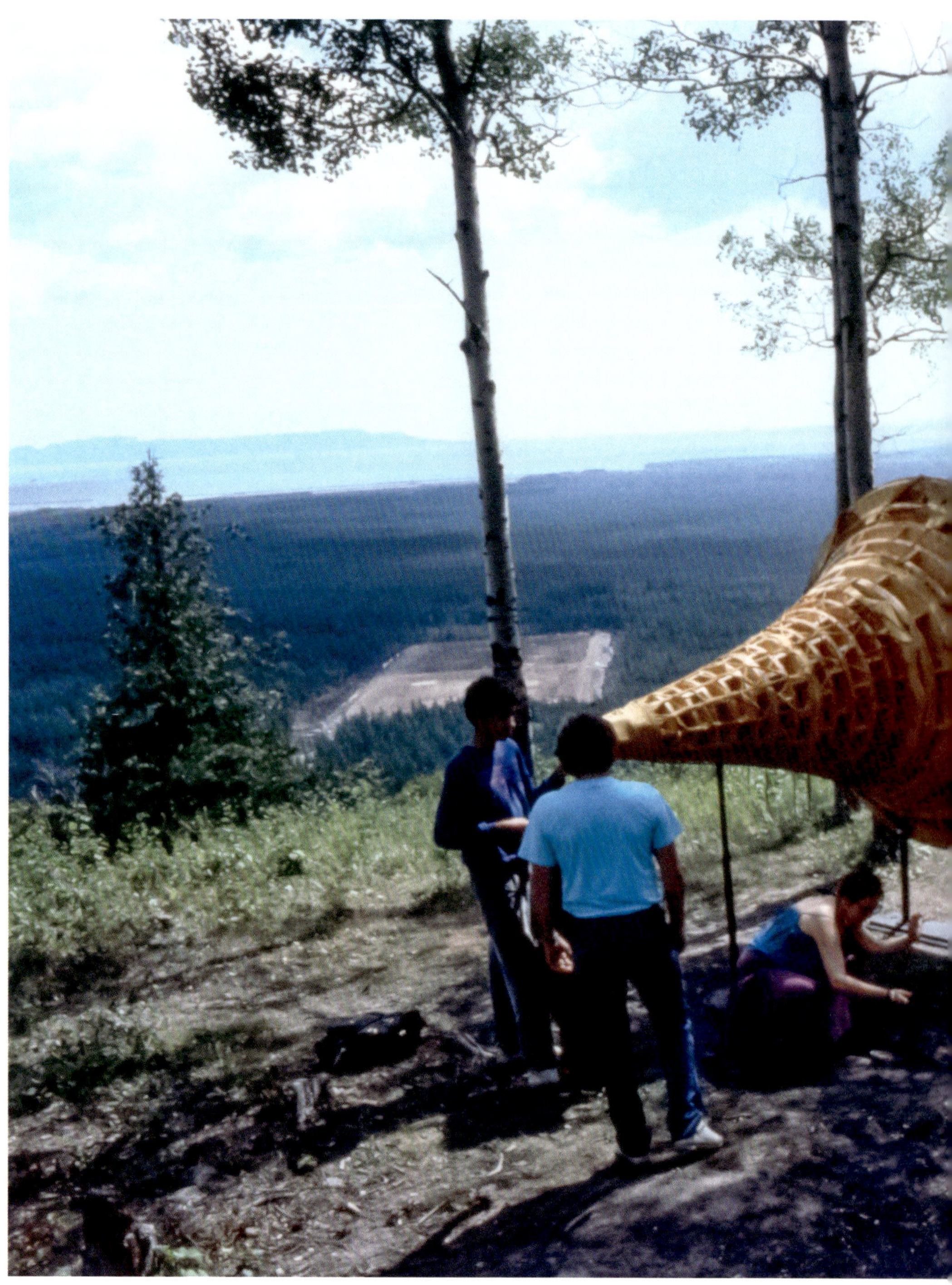

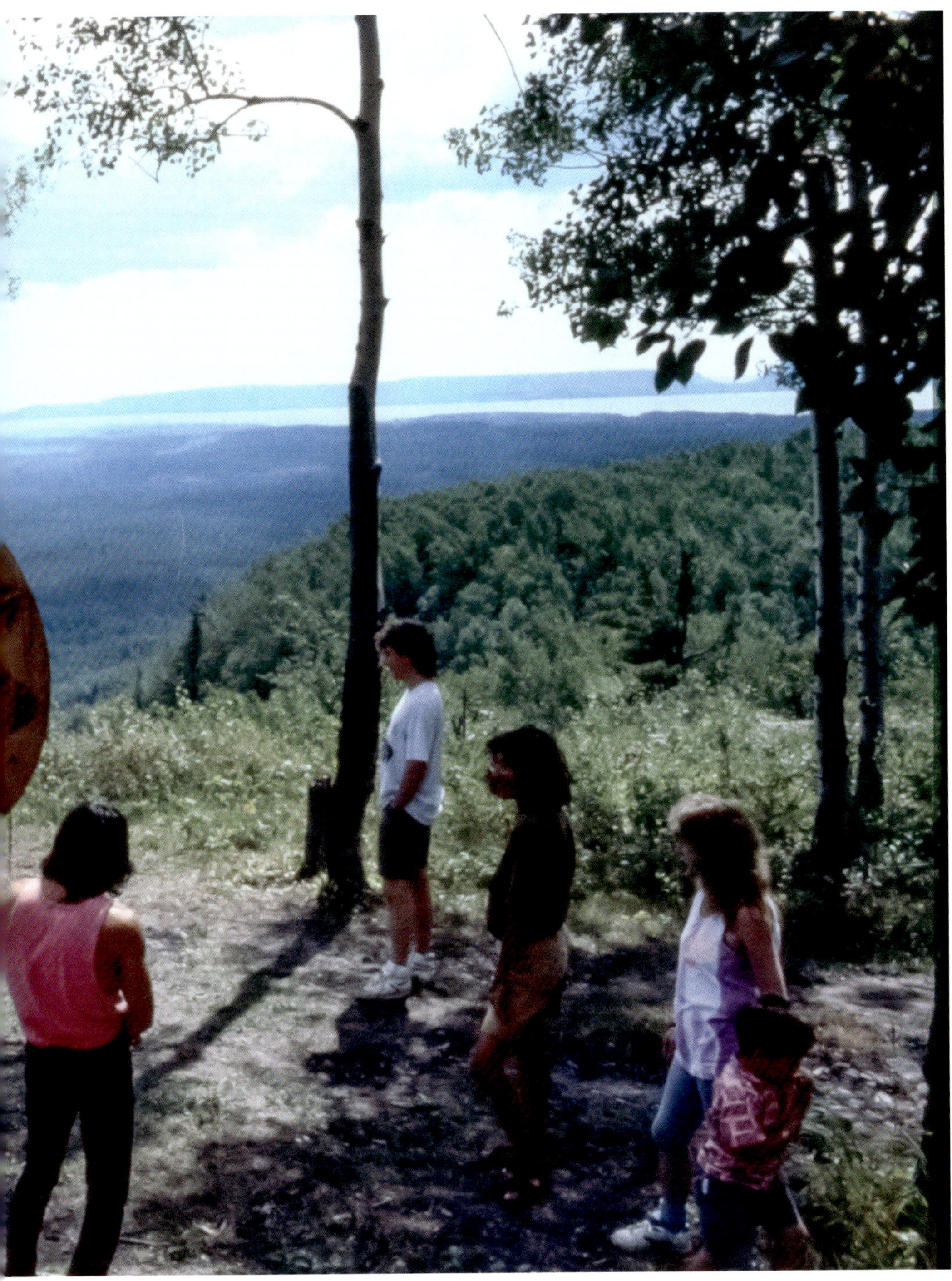

skills," and then "in a critique I was criticized for using my culture. And I thought what the fuck am I supposed to be talking about. I was just an Indian but also the life and times of America. I started looking at my own experiences as a Native American. The good things and the bad things." Luna took a performance class and observed, "I found a medium that I could express what was simmering in my soul. I never looked back."[18] Their experiences of not finding space to do the work they thought necessary made them both quit art school. Luna eventually went back and finished his degree at the University of California, Irvine, and proceeded to settle in his traditional territory of La Jolla in 1976. A decade later, Belmore chose not to finish art school, moving back to Thunder Bay in northern Ontario, near where she grew up. These experiences tell you a lot about the art world values and curricula of the 1970s and '80s and the place of Natives within it.

Luna and Belmore turned these educational, lived "lessons" about the boundaries of the art world into fuel for their self-determined art practices, often taking their work to the streets, to the people, and into other non-museum spaces. By 1992 both had created a body of work that museums and galleries had a great desire to exhibit. That year—1992—marks the full-blown extension of an Indigenous-centered, embodied sense of history coming to the fore. As the world celebrated the five hundredth anniversary of the landing of Christopher Columbus and the birth of the so-called West in the Americas, Indigenous peoples were primed to take over the narrative and impress upon the public that they were effectively marking five centuries of colonialism. Artists utilized the growing interest in Indigenous perspectives to rewrite nationalist narratives of triumph. For example,

18 "Diversity Lecture Series, Spring 2008: James Luna," posted November 8, 2011, by The Evergreen State College, YouTube, https://www.youtube.com/watch?v=4NBpkNxJS9E.

← Fig. 4 Rebecca Belmore (Anishinaabe), *Ayum-ee-aawach Oomama-mowan: Speaking to Their Mother*, 1991–, sound installation and sculpture with wood and megaphone, performed in various locations in Canada and the United States

Jackson Rushing devoted an issue of *Art Journal* to Native art and summarized the project thus: "The retrospective gaze demanded by Columbus-as-Spectacle, even if it produces a desire for a much-needed 'Indian-centered' history, prevents us from focusing on the continuity of colonization and commodification of Native culture(s) by Euro-American corporate and political interests."[19]

By 1992, many people like Rushing were redefining the arts from within Indigenous-centered histories and producing profound critiques of commodification and colonialism. Jaune Quick-to-See Smith was on the board of the College Art Association (CAA). Robert Houle cocurated an exhibition of contemporary Native art at the National Gallery of Canada. James Luna with the work *Take a Picture of a Real Indian* was included in the Whitney Biennial (fig. 3). Richard Hill and Luna hosted a session at CAA in Chicago called "Everybody Needs an Indian: Native Needs Beyond 1992"; it challenged the art world to stay committed to Native art and artists based on what they actually needed, instead of their momentary use value for Eurocentric events. And Belmore, alongside her sister Florene and partner Michael Beynon, drove her sculpture *Ayum-ee-aawach Oomama-mowan: Speaking to Their Mother* (1991–) across Canada (fig. 4). This work was created in response to the Oka Crisis, in which a group of Kanien'kéha (Mohawk) men, women, and children used their own bodies to stop a neighboring town from turning their sacred pines into a golf course. Belmore's sculpture—a large wood structure based on a cross between a moose call device and a megaphone—amplified the voice of the speaker when activated. The artist invited people to speak directly to the land, taking the work to the steps of the Parliament of Canada and to the communities of Kanesatake, Thunder Bay, Sioux Lookout, Regina, Fort Qu'Appelle, and Meadow Lake. Instead of speaking through or to Western institutions, she made an instrument of direct communication with the real power they were defending: Mother Earth.[20]

19
Jackson Rushing, "Editor's Statement: Critical Issues in Recent Native American Art," *Art Journal* 51, no. 3 (1992): 6.

20
The Oka Crisis made international news because the Canadian government sent armed forces to intervene. The land defenders lasted seventy-eight days against the Canadian state and its apparatuses of violence. Protests in support of the Kanien'kéha were held across North America and Belmore's megaphone became part of this movement. The sound echoes back to the speaker as if the land is responding. See Florene Belmore, *Wordless: The Performance Art of Rebecca Belmore* (Grunt Gallery, 2019), 64.

—

From 1987 to 1992, the perceived shift from artifact to contemporary artist was realized through the hard work of many Indigenous artists. For their embodied practices, Belmore and Luna deserve special recognition for their roles. Sadly the transformations taking place in the 1980s and '90s had only to await the backlash of being called "identity politics." Another essay would be required to parse out this problematic name for the many embodied practices working against or in parallel to Eurocentric art histories. In these pages, I instead pursued a thought experiment. I have asked how artworks and the artists who created them intervene in cemented art histories and bring into being new understandings of and trajectories for the boundaries of art.

Different bodies and cultures have been placed within and outside of Eurocentric art histories, allowing for access into the contemporary that actively creates new art histories. I took 1987 as a moment to examine a tremendous shift in the place of Indigenous art within contemporary art. Our placement as "outside" time needed to shift. We had to be seen as contemporaneous first. From 1987 to 1992, two of the most well-known and prolific Indigenous artists created performances that embodied sovereignty within their practices as a lived reality, rather than something external to our everyday lives. With actions that brought to life Indigenous ways of seeing and being, Belmore drew a line in the snow as Luna drew one in the sand.

"I refuse": Estevão Silva

Lorraine Mendes
& Igor Simões

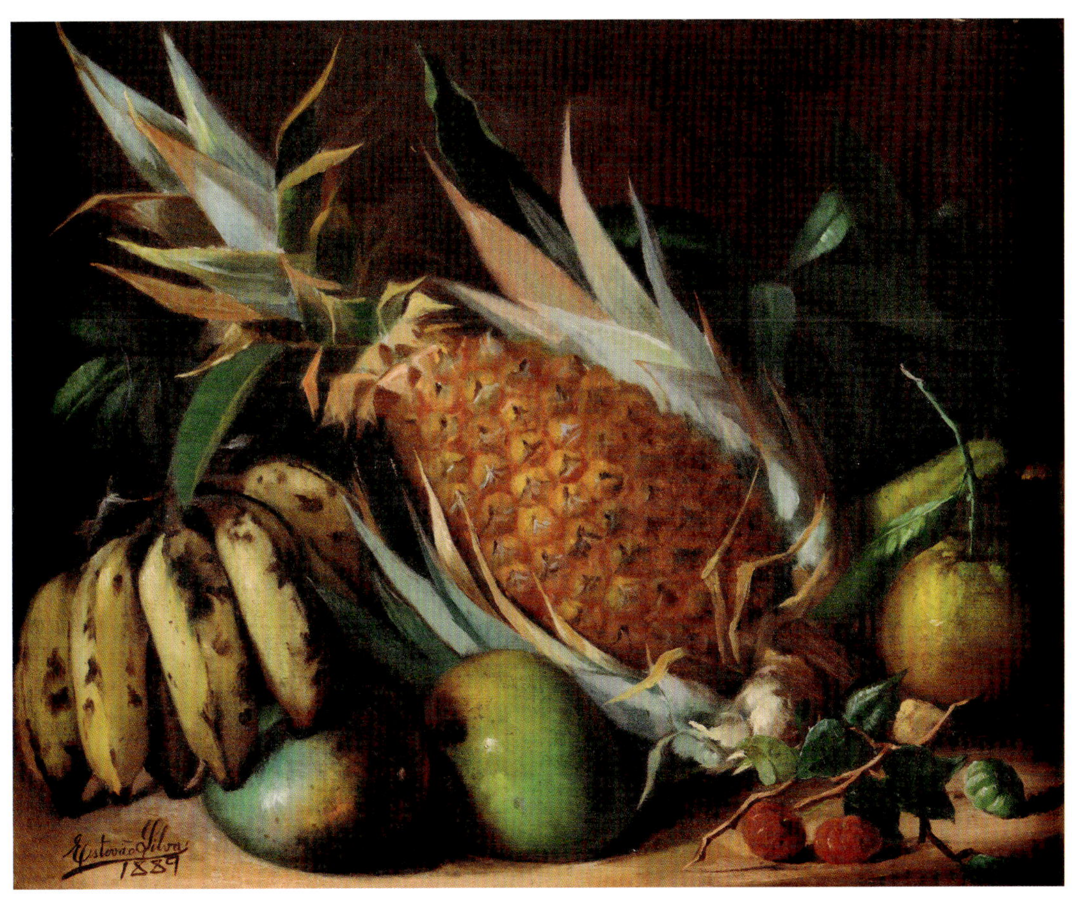
Estevão Silva
1889

An assortment of fruit is on display in a room. Their colors and shapes possess undeniable sensorial appeal. Ripe textures come into view and vivid colors sustain sensuality. We are enthralled by the vibrant pineapple, bananas, mangoes, two delicate pitangas (amid a few green ones)—forms that evoke smells, textures, colors. Their aromas waft through the room. It is as if, for a few seconds, the entire space has been organized to suggest a particular experience, with scents and hues that are specific to one place in the world: Brazil (fig. 1). It is told that a small boy enters the room and devours the fruit with his eyes.[1] He sticks his hand in his pocket and offers a coin to a black man.[2] He wants to take a piece of fruit. There is but one detail that we must reveal: these fruits are, actually, a painting. But not just any painting. We stand before the incomparable still life that emerges through the ability and pictorial rigor of the aforementioned black man.

His name is Estevão Silva (fig. 2). Not by chance, the artist, born and deceased in the nineteenth century, is to this day one of the most important names in art produced in this part of the world, called Brazil. In Brazilian lands, the genre is called *natureza-morta*, from the French *nature morte*, referring to the practice that from its beginning was associated with the painting of inanimate objects (fig. 3). Nevertheless, in the Dutch tradition that is

← Fig. 1 Estevão Silva, *Natureza-morta* (*Still Life*), 1889, oil on canvas, 46 × 54.5 cm, Collection Museu Nacional de Belas Artes/Ibram

adopted in Anglophone countries, the term used is still life. In other words: In lieu of nature being closer to death, there was life that paused and surrendered to the painter's exercise. In Estevão's practice, the idea of life gained another ingredient: During exhibitions, he customarily arranged real fruit—in various stages of maturation—behind his paintings, emphasizing the experience that begins with vision and completes itself in an ambiance that plays with different senses.[3]

In the words of writer Gonzaga Duque, the principal figure in Brazilian criticism during this period, Estevão's paintings are described thus:

> mangoes, the luscious mangoes, that, in [José de] Alencar's opinion, so influenced a sweetening of Brazilian pronunciation: They are warm yellow, bathed in ruby red. Picked in time. Well ripened. Figs, beautiful figs, hear ye, savory, dark colored, descending to the color of Azores red wine. A cluster of tucum coconuts, similar in form and in coloring to the magnificently flavorful black grapes of the Douro. Pink jambo fruit, velvety peaches, blushing carmine, tender araçás, scarlet sectioned pitangas, and an opened papaya carved in half, fruit that is bland to the delicate palate, much as it may be beloved by small singing birds...[4]

Fig. 2 Portrait of Estevão Silva, unknown date, Museu Afro-Brasil

Fig. 3 Estevão Silva, *Natureza-morta* (*Still Life*), 1888, oil on canvas, 37 × 48.5 cm, Pinacoteca do Estado de São Paulo

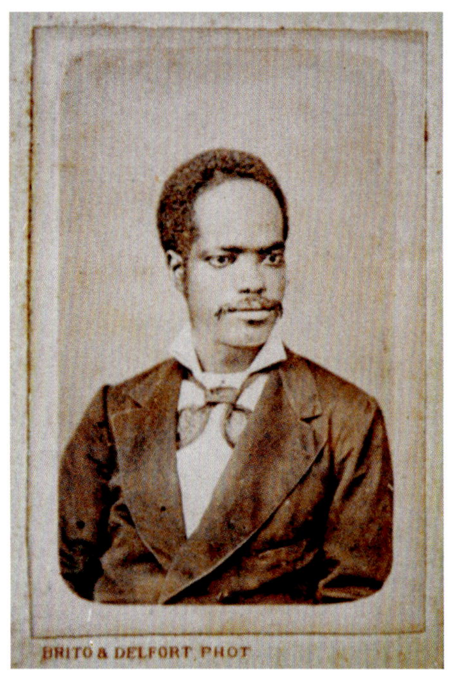

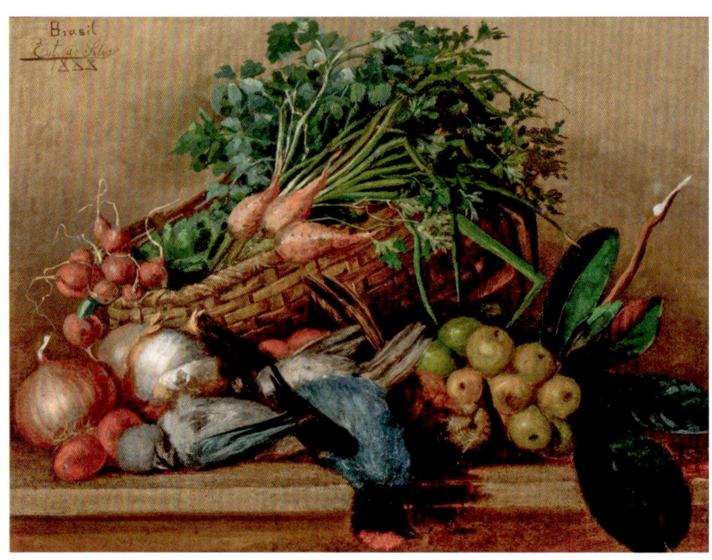

With his palette of colors and deep knowledge of eighteenth-century codes of pictorial representation, Estevão is Brazil's most prominent name in still-life painting. But his contributions surpass the excellence he bestows upon the genre and extend to the larger history of Brazilian art. We will approach these contributions throughout this essay, which is written from a black Brazilian point of view that situates the artist in an essential place debating black art in all the Atlantic.

Estevão is indispensable to the consideration of Afro-Diasporic art production. In gathering the codes apprehended from European academic heritage to risk its legacy in the art of the largest country of the African Diaspora, comprehension of his work is simultaneously yoked to the particular Brazilian racial context and to the set of forms that grow out of experiences that took place within the cultural communities formed during the crossing of the Atlantic Ocean.

Estevão was born in Rio de Janeiro the day after Christmas in 1845, forty-three years before the promulgation of a law that would theoretically abolish slavery in Brazil, where the Atlantic slave trade was conducted for longer than anywhere else in the Americas. In legal documents, he is described as descending from Africans. It cannot be ascertained whether his parents were free or enslaved. Estevão died in November 1891—three years after the act that formally and legally granted freedom to all black people in Brazilian territory.

Of the many fictions that invented Brazil, this freedom for all black people may be the most successful, and one that continues to generate consequences that culminate in hierarchies, divisions, and violence based on the equally fictional idea of race. Two complementary myths come to mind when we think of Brazil. The first is the myth of the three races: to wit, Indigenous, European, and African. It is precisely in Carl Friedrich Philipp von Martius's 1845 text, published in the year of Estevão's birth, that the metaphor of the three rivers is developed,

1
Manoel Carneiro, *Diário Ilustrado. Belas-Artes*, July 21, 1887, 1, in Cristina Pierre França, "A pintura de Estevão Silva e sua relação com a brasilidade," *Encontro de História da Arte* 3 (2007): 241–249.

2
We deliberately do not capitalize the *b* in black as this is not a convention that carries over to the word *negro* in the Brazilian and Latin American contexts, as well as in the Spanish and Portuguese languages.

3
We have maintained here a characteristic of Brazilian Portuguese by referring to the artist by his given name.

4
Gonzaga Duque, *A Semana. Belas-Artes*, no. 126 (May 28, 1887): 4.

used to explain the formative process of the Brazilian people.[5] According to the German naturalist, the white race, specifically of Portuguese blood, was a powerful river that absorbed two small tributaries, which he calls the Indian and Ethiopian races. The admixture would take place in the lowest classes and would become an object of study for historians who dedicated themselves to writing the history of Brazil.

The second myth that interests us here is that of racial democracy. According to Abdias Nascimento, racial democracy is the name of what he calls "imperialism of whiteness and of the capitalism inherent to it."[6] Responsible for upholding the preservation of power by the white supremacist elite, the idea of racial democracy functions as a colonialist device: In the illusion and invention of a harmonious society among races, there would be no racism against which to struggle. Nonetheless, like Martius's metaphor of the three rivers, the concept of racial democracy historically retains the idea that the African and his descendants are inferior. Just as the river of white/European/Portuguese blood was meant to absorb the two smaller ones (in size and in depth), racial democracy subtly suggests assimilation, acculturation, and miscegenation in such a way as to deny and erase the culture and civilizational values of Indigenous peoples and African blacks within the territory that has been stipulated as Brazil.

Although Estevão has not received the attention he deserves in his own country, Brazilian studies on him do exist.[7] Some of them are considerably exhaustive. Yet there is a scarcity of texts and research that introduce the framing we propose here: a historical reading of Estevão, specifically based on the racial paradigm and its unavoidable presence in any attempt at understanding the history of Afro-Diasporic art. It may sound odd that—although Brazil has the largest percentage of black people in any country outside the African continent, making up 55.2 percent of its population, and was the

5
Karl Friedrich Philipp von Martius, "Como se deve escrever a História do Brasil," *Revista do Instituto Histórico e Geográfico Brasileiro* 24, no. 6 (January 1845).

6
Abdias Nascimento, *O genocídio do negro brasileiro: Processo de um racismo mascarado*, 3rd ed. (Perspectiva, 2016).

7
Emanuel Araújo, ed., *A mão afro-brasileira. Significado da contribuição artística e histórica*, vol. 2, 2nd ed. (Imprensa Oficial do Estado de São Paulo/Museu Afro Brasil, 2010); França, "A pintura de Estevão Silva," 241–249; José Roberto Teixeira Leite and Emanoel Araújo, eds., *Pintores Negros do oitocentos* (MWM Motores Diesel, 1988); Heloísa Pires Lima, "A presença negra no circuito da Academia Imperial de Belas Artes do Rio de Janeiro—a década de 80 do século XIX" (master's thesis, Universidade de São Paulo, 2000); Anna Carolina Carlota Mires, "O artista negro na Academia Imperial de Belas Artes: O Legado de Estevão da Silva" (undergraduate thesis, Universidade Federal do

principal destination of the African Diaspora—an Afrocentric approach to one of its greatest artists is rare.

Nevertheless, we speak of an asymmetrical, structurally racist country, one that echoes the colonial process in establishing one of the most perverse notions of whiteness. It is a whiteness that, in its strategies for maintaining privileges, produced a notion of knowledge that considered the racial minority as the center; based on this perversion, it created an idea of Brazilian art that excludes or relegates black artists and theorists to the peripheries. In systemic terms, this approach has been theorized as white Brazilian art.[8]

—

Estevão Silva was the first black man to graduate from the Academia de Belas Artes (Academy of Fine Arts) to achieve historical importance. As was customary in the Americas, the institution grew out of the colonial principle that conquered territories should import artistic codes that were more in keeping with a Eurocentric idea of civilization. In Brazil, the academy opened its doors in 1826, reliant upon a teaching staff made up of French "masters" who were welcomed to the country following their escape from Napoleonic France. These artists would guarantee the imposition of codes that, in many ways, already flirted with anachronism in regard to their European model. Nevertheless, such was the aesthetic program intended to educate the good taste of the former Portuguese colony.[9] Estevão entered the institution in 1863, when he was seventeen. It should be highlighted that he complied with the minimum condition required by the academy in its bylaws: the ability to read, write, and count. This becomes an important detail for, on one hand, it helps us to understand the black presence and literacy in nineteenth-century Brazil and, on the other, the profile of this academy in the Global South. As noted at the time, the Brazilian

Rio de Janeiro, 2019); Alexandre Neiva Pessôa, "Estevão Silva e a pintura de naturezas mortas no Brasil do século XIX" (dissertation, Universidade Federal do Rio de Janeiro, 2002); Letícia Squeff, "Um maldito na Academia: Estevão Silva—algumas notas sobre os caminhos da modernidade no Rio de Janeiro de fins do século XIX," in *Cultura e poder entre o Império e a República: Estudos sobre os imaginários brasileiros (1822–1930)*, ed. Ana Beatriz Demarchi Barel and Wilma Peres Peres (Alameda, 2018), 201–221.

8
Kleber Antônio de Oliveira Amancio, "A história da arte branco-brasileira e os limites da humanidade negra," *Revista Farol* 17, no. 24 (2021); Igor Simões, "Dos Brasis: Para histórias da arte que sejam brasileiras de fato, ou A farsa da arte branco-brasileira, ou Os negros estão aqui," in *Dos Brasis: Arte e pensamento negro*, ed. Igor Simões, Lorraine Mendes, and Marcelo Campos (Sesc São Paulo, 2023).

9
Helena Cunha de Uzeda, "O ensino de arquitetura no contexto da Academia Imperial de Belas Artes do Rio de Janeiro: 1816–1889" (master's thesis, Universidade Federal do Rio de Janeiro, 2000); Cybele Vidal Neto Fernandes, "Os caminhos da arte. O ensino artístico na Academia Imperial das Belas Artes—1850/1890" (PhD diss., Universidade Federal do Rio de Janeiro, 2001).

academy typically catered to the masses, given that public office, medicine, law, and engineering were reserved for the elite. Thus, an idea took shape that Brazilian art of this period came from semiliterate people—and this will recur as an element mentioned by those who, in using Eurocentric parameters, assert the limitations of local art.

Nevertheless, in order to consider Estevão in that institution, we must understand the intersections of class and race in nineteenth-century Brazil, and even today. Since the nineteenth century, race has been the element that overrides class in Brazil. Thus, even among impoverished people, the lowest place in the social structure is reserved for black Brazilians. In this way, although the academy was a place for poor students, it was not necessarily a place for black ones.

Three of the most well-known Afro-Brazilian artists of the period are associated with the Academia de Belas Artes. Following Estevão's admission in 1863, the following years saw the arrival of Firmino Monteiro (1855–1888), who entered the academy in 1873, and Rafael Pinto Bandeira (1863–1896), who arrived in 1879. This was the same year as the notorious scene at the academy's award ceremony, one of the most disseminated moments of Estevão's life. Consequently, it is worth noting that, during the ceremony in question—analyzed in the pages to follow, and of such importance to Estevão's trajectory—Firmino and Rafael were also attending the institution. This remains an open path for examining forms of black sociability in a predominantly white institution.

From very early on, Estevão was singled out by his colleagues as one of the best artists of his time. His friend and colleague, the painter Antonio Parreiras, describes Estevão's talents and the academy's award ceremony in his autobiography:

Fig. 4 Estevão Silva, *Grumixamas e Jaboticabas* (*Grumixamas and Jaboticabas*), n.d., oil on canvas, 44 × 35 cm

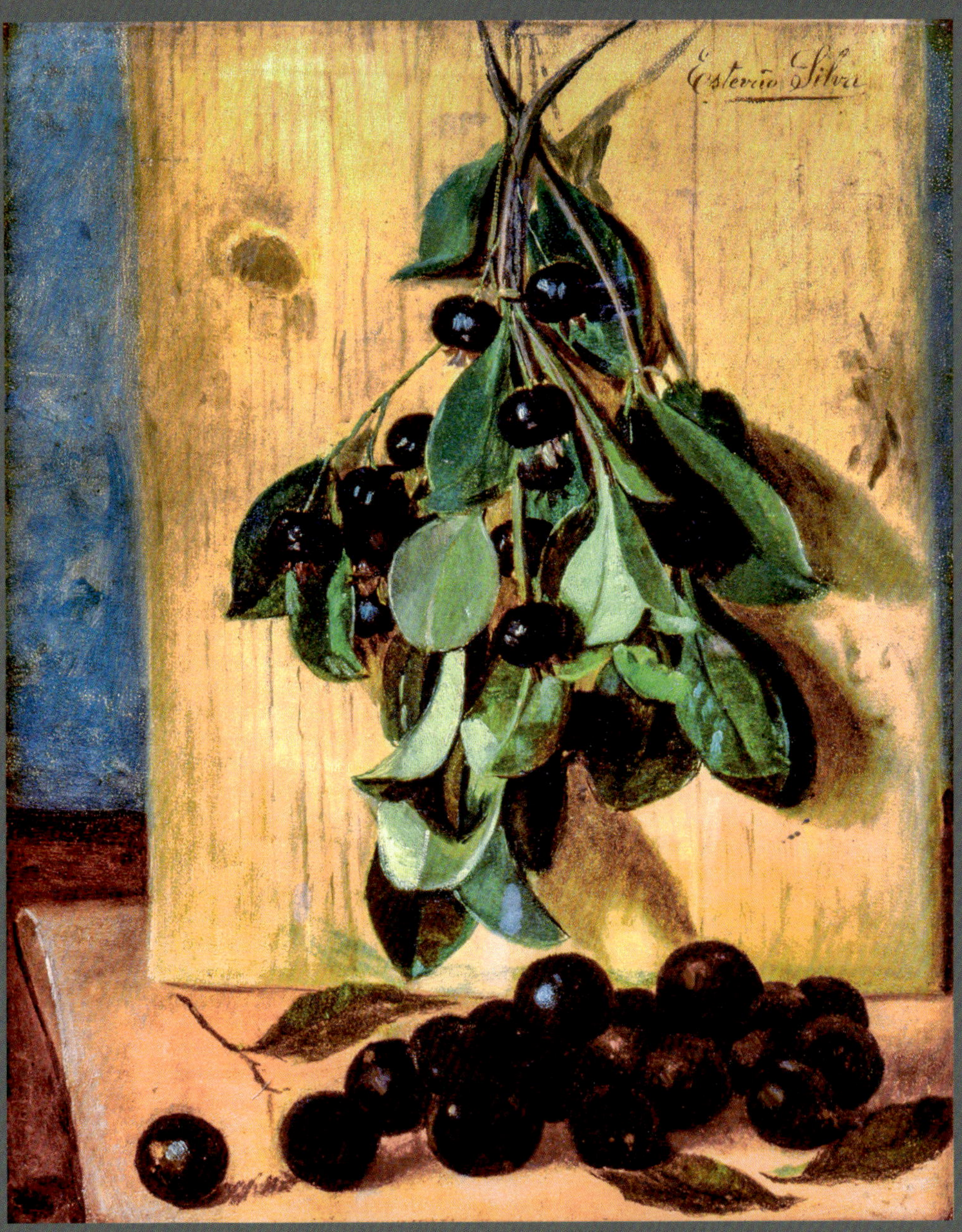

> Thus, there could be no doubt. Estevão would be victorious. This was predicted by all. Estevão's work was the best and unanimously recognized as such by his colleagues. It was with utmost confidence that Estevão awaited the day of the award ceremony, certain that his would be the most important.[10]

Examples of the importance of Estevão's contribution to painting may be found in minute details that demonstrate the rigor, commitment to technique, and subtleties typical of a nineteenth-century virtuouso black Brazilian painter.

Amid his lush still lifes, there is an extremely delicate example whose modest dimensions reveal something of the genius of Estevão himself (fig. 4). In *Grumixamas and Jaboticabas*, an undated oil painting, we see two portions of the small fruits that give the work its title. Grumixama comes from the Tupi word *komixã*, meaning fruit that possesses a sticky or zesty flavor when eaten. Native to the Atlantic Forest, it may be found from the south of Bahia all the way to Rio Grande do Sul, collecting different names along the way that account for its rounded shape, sweetness, texture, and color, which are very similar to those of the jaboticaba. From the Tupi *iawotikáwa*, jaboticaba means "budding fruit," alluding to the way in which it grows directly from the trunk. The grumixama is still commonly described in terms of its similarity to the jaboticaba, which makes the painting all the more curious: With their proximity, we perceive the differences between the two fruits. One is found hanging from branches, with its characteristically small flowering protuberance, and the other is presented on a table, picked from a tree. In this painting, the artist's ability reveals itself in the minute recognition of similar but different details. In Estevão's still lifes, we find traces of a reflection on what Brazilian-ness might be. His composition pairs fruits that were immediately recognizable

10
Antonio Parreiras, *História de um pintor contada por ele mesmo*, 3rd ed. (1926; Niterói Livros, 1999), 50–51.

to Brazilians as well as offering a painstaking study of each species, a visual combination of two of the painter's well-known qualities: excellence and daring.

—

During the traditional ceremony of the Academia de Belas Artes, awards were given to outstanding students, whose works were presented in its general exhibitions.[11] The ceremony included the presence of the emperor of Brazil—at the time, Dom Pedro II—who, within a setting built by members of the academy, was seated on an ornamented throne, from which he announced the winners and awarded medals. The highest award was usually a voyage abroad, most often to Italy and France, where the winning artist could spend time, according to the criteria of the age, perfecting his craft with imperial subsidy. As suggested by Parreiras, there was no doubt that it would be Estevão's year. However, contrary to all predictions, when the awards were announced, Estevão did not win first place, receiving the silver medal instead.

Narrated by Parreiras, the scene is powerfully affective in nature:

> We were convinced that the first prize would be bestowed upon Estevão Silva. Trembling and moved, he waited. But someone else was distinguished by the congregation. Estevão was annihilated. He hung his head, his eyes filled with tears. He flinched and went off to stand behind all the others. We were about to rebel. "Silence! I know what I need to do." So imperiously were the words uttered by that weeping man that we obeyed. One by one, other prizewinners were called. Finally, the name of Estevão Silva echoed throughout the room. He passed calmly among us. He slowly crossed the hall. He approached the platform upon which the emperor was seated.

11
The ceremony could not be described as "annual" as financial difficulties prevented its occurrence during certain years. Thus we have used the word "traditional."

> After that (beautiful, O! Very beautiful), he arrogantly raised his head and loudly shouted: "I refuse."[12]

This act, so often alluded to in descriptions of the artist, affords us a glimpse into the ways that Estevão's history is narrated. As a result of his act of refusal, Estevão was punished by the academy with a yearlong suspension. Some art historians draw our attention to the fact that, considering its rigorous code of conduct, the institution in fact applied a lenient penalty.[13] Nevertheless, from a racialized perspective, it is impossible not to highlight certain sentences in the academy's evaluation, in which the institution itself recognizes that, although outrageous, the artist's action was not in bad faith:

> But hearing the delinquent's defense, the commission was convinced that, due to his modest intelligence...that student who, due to manifestly limited comprehension...taking into account the mitigating circumstance of the delinquent student's intellectual defect.[14]

Among the terms deployed in the academy's assessment, "rebellious," "joker," "unreasonable," and "temperamental" may be found, describing the unfairly treated artist as unintelligent and incapable.

These terms and adjectives are not unknown to black people of different periods. In the case of Brazil, they are very often invoked in representations of the black man across various platforms, in the newspapers reporting racist attacks throughout the country, in recreational racism that disguises the eternal mark of inferiority as a joke. If, nowadays, black bodies such as ours are continued targets for these classifications, let us imagine what it meant in the nineteenth century to be a black artist who dared to be defiant, an artist whose excellence allowed him to recognize his own qualities and particularities in himself.

12
Parreiras, *História de um pintor*.

13
Such is the case with art historian José Roberto Teixeira Leite, who coedited a book about black artists of the nineteenth century, *Pintores Negros do oitocentos* (1988), with artist, curator, and museum director Emanoel Araújo.

14
Adriana Apud Caló, "Resgate de memória: Quem foi Estevão Silva?," *Obvious*, 2015.

We cannot forget that Estevão's act was that of a free black man frequenting white spaces. Further, it occurred at the exact moment when Brazil, in an attempt to uphold its fiction of white heritage and destiny, launched programs that incentivized the immigration of mostly Italian and German men and women to Brazil.[15] These state-financed programs aimed to whiten a Brazilian society made up of a majority of black subjects. This was one of the tactics that, extending through the early decades of the twentieth century, intended to erase the black portion of the population in, at most, three generations, using miscegenation as a guiding principle. Here—contrary to what we see within the context of the United States—miscegenation was part of a strategy in which the *mestiços* born of these unions represent the first steps of a country that coveted whiteness.

Estevão, like Firmino Monteiro and Rafael Pinto Bandeira, black men who lived in Rio de Janeiro during the same period, participated in processes of black resistance that supported the abolitionist movement. This included the promulgation of the Law of Free Birth (or the Rio Branco Law; 1871), which declared all children of enslaved people born from that moment on to be free. Although flawed in its objectives, the law was the subject of a sketch for a historical painting by Estevão, which—along with twenty-three works comprising portraits, landscapes, allegories, and, obviously, still lifes—was presented by the artist at the 26th General Exhibition (1884).[16] Thus, contrary to common belief, Estevão's production was not limited to still lifes but rather extended to all genres of academic painting. It should be noted that within the hierarchy of academic genres, still life occupied the lowest level, being considered a component rather than a goal of the artist's training. Nevertheless, as is the case in other Latin American contexts, the still life and the portrait were the principal means of support for artists; they were less frequently supported in pursuing history painting, the more celebrated academic genre.

15
Luiza Horn Iotti, *Imigração e colonização: Legislação de 1747–1915* (Assembleia Legislativa do Estado do RS, 2001); Beatriz Maria Lazzari, *Imigração e ideologia: Reação do parlamento brasileiro à política de colonização e imigração (1850–1875)* (Escola Superior de Teologia São Lourenço de Brindes, 1980).

16
Sirlene Alves and Alexandra Lima da Silva, "O voo das graúnas: Estudantes negras/os como intelectuais," *Revista Brasileira de História de Educação* 22 (2022). One of Silva's landscapes was acquired by the academy itself.

Fig. 5 Estevão Silva, *Retrato do pintor Giovanni Battista Castagneto* (*Portrait of Painter Giovanni Battista Castagneto*), 1880, oil on canvas, 45.5 × 37.2 cm, Collection Museu Nacional de Belas Artes/Ibram

Fig. 6 Estevão Silva, *Retrato de Castagneto* (*Portrait of Castagneto*), c. 1885, oil on cardboard, 57 × 48 cm, Collection Pinacoteca do Estado de São Paulo

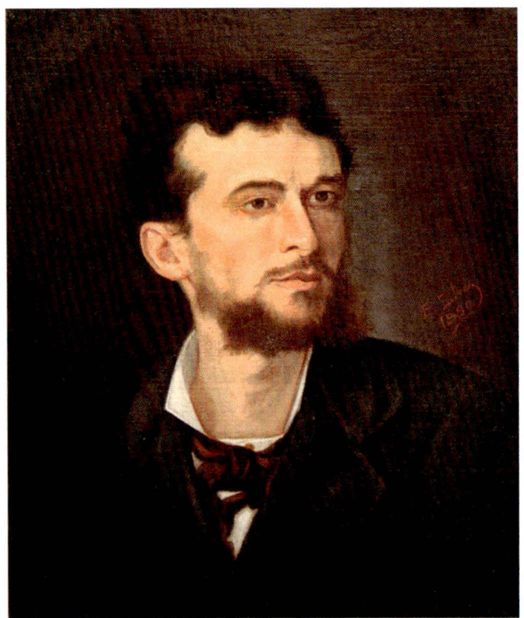

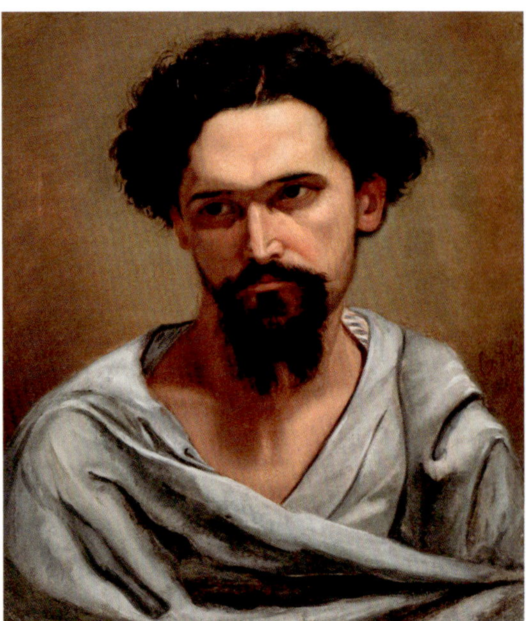

Simultaneously, due to external impositions, principally in the economic field, Brazil was obliged to produce an international image that was closer to modern liberal values and distant from that of a slaveholding country. By no coincidence, only one year after the "definitive" end of slavery, Estevão was the artist with the largest number of works in the Brazilian Pavilion at the Paris world's fair of 1889.[17] With his paintings of Brazilian fruit, Estevão presented the wealth of national development even as he contributed to the international messaging of a country in which blacks were not only free, but also had a prominent place in society. This mirage never materialized.

—

Deceased in 1891, Estevão was never freed from the essentialist and reductionist concepts of Brazilian society, not even in the well-deserved tributes paid to his career. On the occasion of the artist's passing, the aforementioned white Brazilian critic Gonzaga Duque wrote an obituary emphasizing the artist's greatness:

> **Whosoever, like him, is descended from an uncultivated oppressed race and has been oppressed, and has struggled,** does not possess the dull, difficult, meandering, winding nebulosity of the refined, **will always see bloodred, will always desperately see yellow.** Let us now note the sharp contrast of the shadows whose color he would never manage to lose, despite the heavy, occasionally violent hues with which he imbued his paintings. **He is black without lightness, nor transitions.**[18]

Within the perspective fueled by deterministic philosophers, Gonzaga Duque would have it that Estevão's formal elaborations were the direct result of a sort of

17
Empire du Brésil: Catalogue officiel (Paris, 1889), 18.

18
Gonzaga Duque, "Estevão Silva. Contemporâneos (pintores e escultores), Rio de Janeiro, Typ. Benedicto de Sousa. 1919," from *Mostra do redescobrimento: Negro de corpo e alma*, ed. Nelson Aguilar (Fundação Bienal de São Paulo, 2000), 324–325 (emphasis ours).

ancestral essence that inhabited a subject who, being descended from Africans, would carry within himself the heat and blood of that continent.

Like that of other Afro-Atlantic artists, Estevão's life was shot through with racist concepts that limit readings of his work to a single, repetitive key based on preconceived notions about being black in Europe and the Americas. Beyond the brilliance of his still lifes, which led us to this point, we invite the reader to stand before portraits of the Italian Brazilian artist Castagneto, painted by Estevão on two separate occasions (figs. 5–6). Between the portrait of 1880, more static and firmly classical, and the portrait of circa 1885, in which new-found solutions to the treatment of the sitter, to color, and to space announce more modern readings, what stands out is an artist aware of the codes of canonical art who finds his own authorial particularities. There is no visible sign of the painter being black. It is in this manner that, from the nineteenth century, Estevão continues to point toward paths that are still necessary for black art.

Before an international art system that wishes to foment its fetishes in reiterated representations of black bodies or codes that announce his black origin, Estevão reminds us that a black artist need not necessarily allude to subjects, figurations, or representations that are rapidly associated with a limited repertory of what constitutes blackness. A black artist produces Afro-Brazilian art, black art, or Afro-Diasporic art because it is of his existence in the world, as a descendant of ocean waters, that the challenges imposed to this day upon black bodies are manifested. Afro-Diasporic art is not defined by subjects nor styles. What unites these artists is not an aesthetic category but rather a political one. Afro-Brazilian art or, beyond it, Afro-Diasporic art is sustained by the fact that it is produced by black people who rise up, who refuse the limitations imposed upon them: black artists who rise up defiant. Defiant like Estevão Silva.

Pageantry as Police Work
Seeta Chaganti

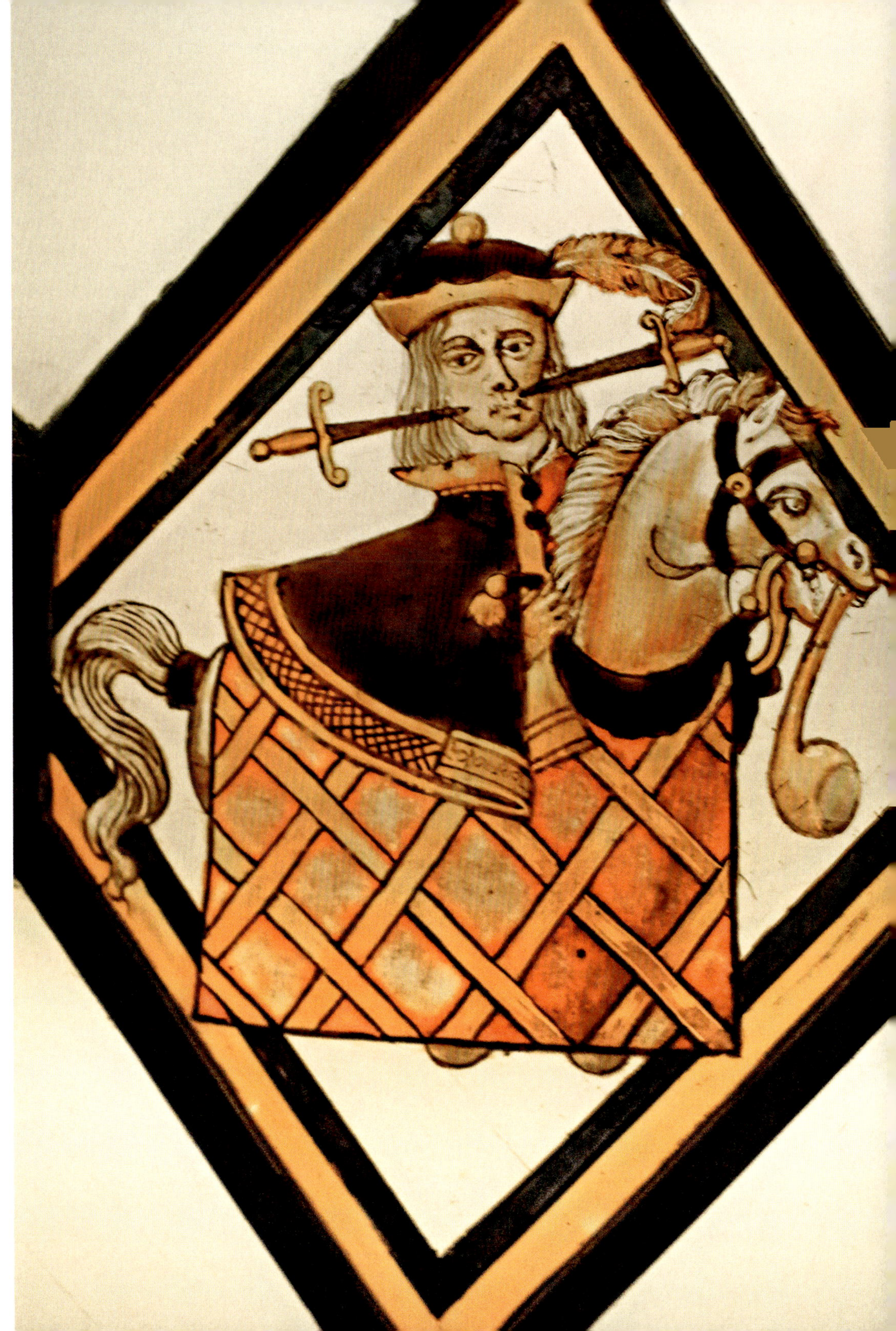

...each of the sheriffs had besides their giants but two pageants, each their morris dance....
—John Stow[1]

Morris dance represents one of the many performance genres for which early modern England—the birthplace of Shakespearean theater—is famous. While little evidence remains to reconstruct the earliest forms of this dance, it involved extravagantly and exotically costumed dancers, often adorned with bells, engaging in possibly antic movements. In sixteenth-century London, morris dances were incorporated into the many civic processions and pageants that showcased the power of both elected municipal officials and visiting royal dignitaries. This performance scenario might not, in itself, strike modern readers as particularly odd; what probably would, however, is the consistent connection between morris dance and the figure of the London sheriff. In these civic spectacles, why was morris dance associated with sixteenth-century London sheriffs?

In answer, this essay suggests that morris dance featured a juristic and racially opportunistic choreography that aligned with the sheriff's most ancient enforcements of law and order. This choreography figured Black, brown, and Muslim persons as conditionally integrated into English rights-based recognition while at the same time excluding them

← Betley Window stained-glass panel (detail), 1621, clear glass painted with colored enamels and yellow paint, Victoria and Albert Museum, C.248-1976

from access to real property possession. Drawing upon historiographical accounts, purchase records, and visual materials, I shall elucidate the message that morris dance conveyed to its early audiences: Within England's green and pleasant land, perpetuating wealthy whiteness meant policing access to land as material futurity for non-white residents. This reading of morris dance supports modern arguments for the abolition of police and all carceral systems. It thus ultimately demonstrates how an abolitionist perspective offers scholars of premodernity a means to advocate for present and future liberation, even when their historical archives uphold a repressive status quo.

—

Of primary importance in the investigation of morris dance is its relationship to the English lexeme *moor*. While early modern European writers produced taxonomies differentiating non-European people of diverse backgrounds from each other, Ambereen Dadabhoy shows that *moor* was at the same time an identity of polysemy.[2] If *moor* could designate North African, sub-Saharan African, Afro-Spanish, Muslim, and Middle Eastern identities, the lexically related *morris* could refer to any number of these. Recent scholarship recognizes the transnational character of English morris, particularly as reflective of Europe's demographic situation in this period. Among the most important examples of this scholarship are works by Michael Heaney and by Noémie Ndiaye. Heaney's account of the history of morris dance mentions Continental dance performances that represent Middle Eastern figures.[3] He furthermore gathers visual evidence that English and northern European morris dance incorporated visual reference to African, Afro-Diasporic, and Middle Eastern peoples from an early moment, citing Erasmus Grasser's figurines portraying dark-skinned and exotically costumed morris dancers before the end of the fifteenth century (figs. 1–2).

Considering such images—the portrayed physiognomies, postures, costumes, and skin colors—requires acknowledging Ndiaye's reminder that "the epistemological limitations of a kinetic archive entirely constituted by white subjectivity" render it impossible for us to know if dances or dancers represented during the early modern period "were genealogically connected to authentic dances" from outside Europe.[4] In the English context, a wooden panel depicts a morris dancer who appears to at least one historian of morris dance, Barbara Lowe, as African (fig. 3).[5] The figure to whom Lowe refers appears in her estimation naked, dancing to the immediate right of the musician, who is possibly a Fool character, and accompanied by four dancers in tunics. Works such as these indicate that morris dance and its Continental relatives were bound in some way to perceptions of African and Islamic worlds. At the same time, per Ndiaye's argument, such depictions' mediation through the white Western lenses of both original artists and modern critical interpreters such as Lowe must be taken into account.

Underlying Ndiaye's analysis is a dichotomy of repression and liberation, one that lays out an important challenge to the present essay. Given the extent to

1
John Stow, *The Survey of London* (1603; E. P. Dutton, 1929), 94.

2
Ambereen Dadabhoy, *Shakespeare Through Islamic Worlds* (Routledge, 2024), 130–136.

3
Michael Heaney, *The Ancient English Morris Dance* (Archaeopress, 2023), 8–10.

4
Noémie Ndiaye, *Scripts of Blackness: Early Modern Performance Culture and the Making of Race* (University of Pennsylvania Press, 2022), 233. Throughout, I follow Ndiaye's orthographic practice, which distinguishes "black," a European and "prescriptive" performance designation, from "Black," a "dynamics of politico-cultural self-identification" (28–29).

5
Barbara Lowe refers to this figure as "a naked black 'girl'" in "Early Records of the Morris in England," *Journal of the English Folk Dance and Song Society* 8, no. 2 (1957): 65.

which white representational practice dictated "artificial prescriptive" conceptions of race in the archive, Ndiaye critiques "the argumentative grammar...which too often construes black oppression as a mere qualifying clause to a main clause foregrounding Black resistance and self-emancipation."[6] She finds a solution to this problem in the agency of "Black performers' documented bids for control over black dances' cultural sites of production."[7] The specific case of sixteenth-century morris dance, however, makes it difficult to confirm unambiguously the presence of Black performers or designers of spectacle. Morris dance thus presents a significant challenge if we hope to read it in a way aligned with a liberatory political project.

Lacking a robust morris archive of Black agency, we have instead only the backdrop of England's racially repressive performance practices, particularly impersonation as a performance practice adjacent to morris. Fifteenth- and sixteenth-century chronicles sometimes connect unspecified dance genres to spectacles of racial impersonation. Edward Hall's *Chronicle* narrates two scenes within a Westminster court spectacle during Henry VIII's reign. Together, these scenes associate dance with a disguising that represents "Moreskoes":

> The torchebearers were appareyled in Crymosyn satyne and grene, lyke Moreskoes, their faces blacke: And the kyng brought in a momerye.... [The ladies'] faces, neckes, armes & handes, couered with fyne pleasaunce blacke: Some call it Lumberdynes, which is merueylous thine, so that thesame ladies semed to be nygrost or blacke Mores. Of these foresayed. vi. ladyes, the lady Mary, syster vnto the kyng was one, the other I name not. After that the kygnes grace and the ladies had daunsed a certayne tyme they departed euery one to his lodging.[8]

6
Ndiaye, *Scripts of Blackness*, 26–27.

7
Ndiaye, *Scripts of Blackness*, 191.

8
Edward Hall, *Hall's Chronicle; Containing the History of England* (1548; AMS Press, 1965), 513, 514.

[The torchbearers were appareled in crimson and green satin, like Moorish performers/a Moorish disguising/spectacle, their faces black; And the king brought in a mumming....
The ladies' faces, necks, arms, and hands, covered with fine pleasance [sheer fabric] black. Some call it Lombardine, which is marvelously thin, so that the same ladies seemed to be Negroes or blackamoors. Of these aforementioned six ladies, the lady Mary, sister to the king, was one, the other I do not name. After the king's grace and the ladies had danced a certain time, everyone departed to his own lodging.]

Identifying a practice of blacking up, this passage depicts the integration of dance with costuming through a "Moorish" aesthetic. Based on a record of payment "for playing of the Morrice Dance," Lowe surmises that certain morris dance presentations blurred the lines between dance and other performance. She goes on to note an early sixteenth-century manual specifying that morris dance should follow disguising.[9] Similarly, E. K. Chambers cites a 1559 court masque with impersonations that featured "black lawn" for hair and "black velvet" on faces and limbs, noting that this record's additional reference to bells suggests that "it is probable that a morris was introduced" in this scene.[10] (The use of bells was familiar in Afro-Spanish dance.)[11] Chambers's example supports the possibility of adjoining morris dance in particular to racial impersonation.

These examples point us in turn toward the racializing implications within and beyond costuming in explicit records of morris dance. John Stow names morris dance as a component in the civic pageants and festivals occurring in London throughout the first half of the sixteenth century, in particular May festivals and Watches, the latter a festive allusion to a historical tradition of patrolling by night against possible threat. On May festivals:

9
Lowe, "Early Records of the Morris," 62.

10
E. K. Chambers, *The Elizabethan Stage* (Clarendon Press, 1923), 1:156.

11
Ndiaye, *Scripts of Blackness*, 195.

12
Stow, *Survey of London*, 90, 94.

13
Expenditure lists showing the purchase of costumes for morris dance and "Moorish" appearance appear in the accounts of the Tudor royal Office of Masks and Revels (founded in 1544 but with earlier related documents) as well as in the accounts of livery companies producing civic spectacles. See Albert Feuillerat, ed., *Documents Relating to the Revels at Court in the Time of King Edward VI and Queen Mary (The Losley Manuscripts)* (Kraus Reprint, 1968), e.g., 29–32; as well as the thorough examination of manuscript sources pertaining to civic theater throughout Anne

> in the month of May, the citizens of London of all estates, lightly in every parish, or sometimes two or three parishes joining together, had their several mayings, and did fetch in May-poles, with divers warlike shows, with good archers, morris dancers, and other devices, for pastime all the day long; and toward the evening they had stage plays, and bonfires in the streets.

He further notes:

> The sheriffs' watches came one after the other in like order, but not so large in number as the mayor's; for where the mayor had besides his giant three pageants, each of the sheriffs had besides their giants but two pageants, each their morris dance, and one henchman, their officers in jackets of worsted or say, party-coloured, differing from the mayor's, and each from other, but having harnessed men a great many, etc.[12]

If these passages lack choreographic detail, they correlate with Hall's references to elaborate costuming in his account of unspecified dance. Morris costuming is further apparent in expenditure lists: red and black buckram, and, again, bells.[13] More suggestively, while the record appears to indicate that the black buckram is for coats (*tunicis*), this loosely woven linen could have joined other fabrics used in performance to impersonate dark skin, such as "plesaunce."[14] For Ian Smith, black cloth allowed early modern audiences to limit Black personhood by rendering it as material object.[15] Fabric, he further argues, gestured toward praxes of impersonation whether or not used literally to black up: the handkerchief in *Othello* thus "becomes the highly evocative and comparable image of the white actor's body fitted in dyed black cloth."[16] As this performance dynamic emerged, black fabric juxtaposed with morris could have fulfilled a similar

Lancashire, *London Civic Theatre: City Drama and Pageantry from Roman Times to 1558* (Cambridge University Press, 2002), esp. specific citations below. See also Jean Robertson and D. J. Gordon, *Collections Volume III: A Calendar of Dramatic Records in the Books of the Livery Companies of London, 1485–1640* (Malone Society, 1954), 17, on payment to morris dancers by the Drapers.

14
Ian Smith, "White Skin, Black Masks: Cross-Dressing on the Early Modern Stage," *Renaissance Drama*, n.s., vol. 32 (2003): 44.

15
Smith, "White Skin," 39.

16
Ian Smith, "Othello's Black Handkerchief," *Shakespeare Quarterly* 64, no. 1 (2013): 21.

Fig. 1 Erasmus Grasser, *Morris Dancer with Headdress*, 1480, painted linden wood, h. 63 cm, Münchner Stadtmuseum, Sammlung Angewandte Kunst

Fig. 2 Erasmus Grasser, *Morris Dancer with Lion Motif on Hat*, 1480, painted linden wood, h. 61 cm, Münchner Stadtmuseum, Sammlung Angewandte Kunst

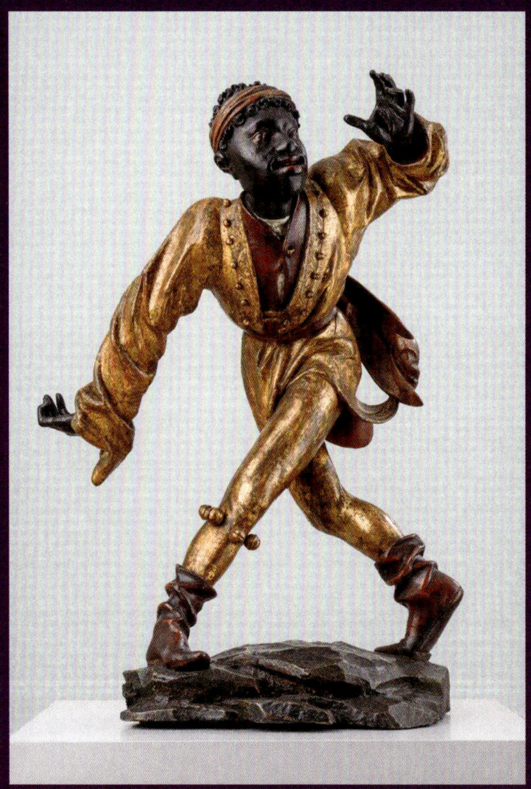

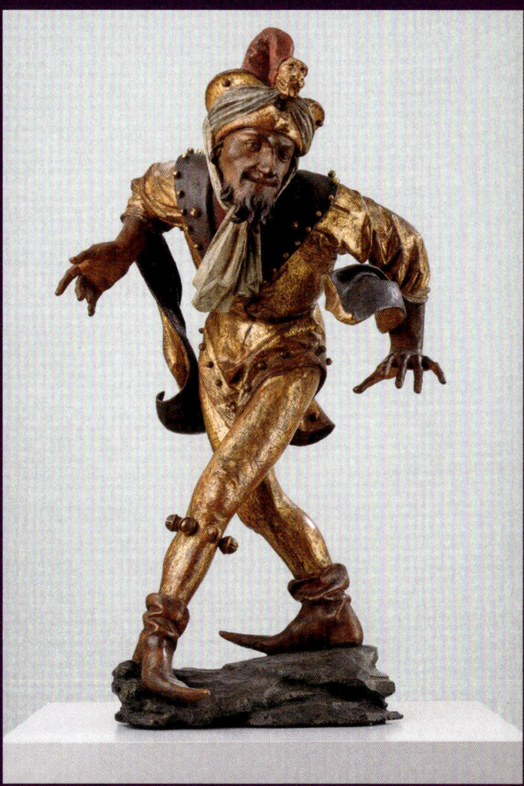

function. Even if morris dancers were not costumed for racial impersonation, the dance itself reflected a racialized character. This racialized character could not only, as Ndiaye suggests, be co-opted by white dancers for their own political purposes but also, I would add, signal racial consciousness for legal and economic agendas.[17]

Alongside the racializing elements of morris dance exist bureaucratic allusions in morris-based testimony. Hall's chronicle mentions a morris dance at Richmond during Epiphany that formed part of a

> pageant deuised like a mountayne, glisteringe by night, as though it had bene al of golde and set with stones, on the top of the which mountayne was a tree of golde, the braunches and bowes frysed with gold, spredynge on euery side ouer the mountayne, with Roses and Pomegranettes…& out of the same came a ladye, appareiled in cloth of golde, and the chyldren of honor called the Henchemen, whiche were freshly disguised, and daunced a Morice before the kyng. And that done, reentered the moutaine [*sic*]…[18]

> [pageant devised like a mountain, glittering by night, as though it had been all of gold and set with stones, on the top of which was a tree of gold, the branches and bows banded with gold, spreading on every side over the mountain, with roses and pomegranates…and out of the same came a lady appareled in cloth of gold, and the children of honor called the henchmen, who were gaily costumed, and danced a morris before the king. And that done, reentered the mountain…]

The "Henchemen" remind us of the role that other city officials—including sheriffs—played in presenting morris dance.[19] Furthermore, in addition to the reference above to sheriffs' pageants and morris dances, Stow's account of

17
Ndiaye, *Scripts of Blackness*, 193, 210–211.

18
Hall, *Hall's Chronicle*, 516–517.

19
Oxford English Dictionary (2019), under "henchman," sense 1a.

the May Day festivities that include morris dance specifies sheriffs attending these events during Henry VI's reign.[20] A late sixteenth-century record shows a county sheriff arranging a feast for legal officials that included payments to minstrels.[21] Sheriffs of sixteenth-century London also tended to be associated with the wealthy guilds that provided support for the morris dances. Normalizing the juxtaposition of law enforcement, feasting, and entertainment, we might explain such governmentally sanctioned festivities by noting that early modern civic pageantry conveyed balance among the commons, the oligarchical elite governing London, and the Crown.[22]

—

But did sheriffs have other species of attachment to morris dance? When the central government condemned morris dance, the sheriff of Oxford protested. He criticized attempts to "abolish," for religious reasons, "pastimes" including morris dance "to the great discontentment of Her Majesty's loving subjects."[23] Earlier, the will of the fifteenth-century sheriff of Nottinghamshire and Derbyshire (as well as member of Parliament), Sir Thomas Chaworth, mentions a silver object "with a Moresk [th]eron," which Heaney speculates, based on references to similar objects, depicts the dance.[24] If it does portray morris dance, this artifact might suggest that a busy, important, late medieval sheriff experienced toward morris the sense of nostalgia or fetish that miniaturization itself can inspire.[25] Given this potential intensity of attachment, perhaps the explanation for the sheriff's morris as mere civic optics does not fully explain his relationship to morris dance. Instead, as the remainder of this essay will demonstrate, morris symbolically conveys the policing of racial minorities' integration into England and the regulation of their access to property possession, both duties associated with the sheriff.

20 Stow, *Survey of London*, 90.

21 Jonathan McGovern, *The Tudor Sheriff: A Study in Early Modern Administration* (Oxford University Press, 2022), 44.

22 On these negotiations, see Ian W. Archer, *The Pursuit of Stability: Social Relations in Elizabethan London* (Cambridge University Press, 1991), 25–30.

23 Heaney, *Ancient English Morris Dance*, 62.

24 Heaney, *Ancient English Morris Dance*, 7. See Kathleen E. Kennedy, "Moors and Moorishness in Late Medieval England," *Studies in the Age of Chaucer* 42 (2020): 216, 243 on "Moresk" decorative lettering.

25 Susan Stewart, *On Longing: Narratives of the Miniature, the Souvenir, the Gigantic, the Collection* (Duke University Press, 1993), 23, 65.

The English sheriff's pre-Conquest history illuminates his role in adjudicating property possession. The sixteenth-century sheriff retained his Germanic name, *scirgerefa* (shire-reeve), and, like his early predecessors, ascertained property boundaries by visiting the location and riding.[26] From the pre-Conquest period, shire courts heard instructions regarding land grants, with sheriffs often among the addressees in these documents.[27] In the transition from Germanic to Norman rule, according to Richard Abels, sheriffs became "critical in overseeing and facilitating the massive redistribution of land that took place between 1066 and 1086."[28] This office's preservation over time accommodates its preoccupation with landholding. At even the etymological level, the term preserves its reference to the *shire*, the land locating the sheriff's duties. These associations may be more than abstract. Henry VIII's dissolution of the monasteries fundamentally altered the nature of the land market. During the sixteenth century, "the English populace probably enjoyed the most widely diffused ownership of modest amounts of individually alienable property in Europe at this time, rendering the issue of inheritance legally problematic for a much greater proportion of the populace than throughout much of the continent," Simon Szreter argues.[29] Preoccupation with alienability, entailment, and conveyance influenced a system of parish recording in this period to safeguard the legal transfer of land.[30] English law furthermore restricted alien acquisition of land or homes at the same time that it made possible circumventions of these rules.[31] A sixteenth-century Florentine merchant, for instance, married an English woman and thus obtained real estate.[32] In an earlier example, a fourteenth-century foreign resident received a grant of protection, described as being similar to denization, which allowed him to acquire lands for his heirs.[33] As the inheritor of an ancestral office enforcing land rights, the sixteenth-century sheriff is the historical weft of a fabric that reflects pervasive, continued preoccupation with land rights for every type of resident.

26
McGovern, *Tudor Sheriff*, 86.

27
Chelsea Shields-Más, "The Sheriffs of Edward the Confessor" *Anglo-Norman Studies* 55 (2023): 65.

28
Richard Abels, "Sheriffs, Lord-Seeking and the Norman Settlement of the South-East Midlands," in *Anglo-Norman Studies: Proceedings of the Battle Conference on Anglo-Norman Studies* (Boydell, 1997), 33.

29
Simon Szreter, "Registration of Identities in Early Modern English Parishes and Amongst the English Overseas," in *Registration and Recognition: Documenting the Person in World History*, ed. Keith Breckinridge and Simon Szreter (Oxford University Press, 2012), 70.

30
Szreter, "Registration of Identities," 75, 88.

31
Keechang Kim, *Aliens in Medieval Law: The Origins of Modern Citizenship* (Cambridge University Press, 2004), 115.

32
Alwyn A. Ruddock, "Alien Merchants in Southampton in the Later Middle Ages," *English Historical Review* 61, no. 239 (1946): 6.

33
Bart Lambert and W. Mark Ormond, "Friendly Foreigners: International Warfare, Resident Aliens, and the Early History of Denization in England, c. 1250–1400," *English Historical Review* 130, no. 542 (2015): 18, 24.

34
Imtiaz Habib, *Black Lives in the English Archives, 1500–1677: Imprints of the Invisible* (Routledge, 2008), 40.

35
Habib, *Black Lives*, 43.

36
Habib, *Black Lives*, 77, 304.

37
E. M. Leonard, *The Early History of English Poor Relief* (Cambridge University Press, 1900), 297n1: "the Attorney-General informed against a certain Negroose and others for building cottages…'contrary to the proclamation.'"

Against this backdrop emerged a population of African and Middle Eastern residents who increasingly participated in English commerce in urban and rural spaces. Some of the following examples derive from Imtiaz Habib's detailed work with parish records; if these records did one kind of work for white English subjects, as suggested above, they revealed something different for non-white residents. The trumpeter John Blanke was, in Habib's reading, "a professional black man," paid and held in "stable esteem" in the early sixteenth century.[34] Peter Negro, knighted in 1547, received a cash award that, Habib speculates, "may also have included other privileges such as an instant denization and land grants, since that is what accompanies such honors given to others."[35] Lambert Waterson, described as "barbaryen," was called "denizen" and "tenaunte."[36] In the late sixteenth century, a Black Londoner was fined for building a cottage that violated the city's size and height regulations.[37] If these examples concern persons embedded in English militia and urban commerce, ambassadorial delegations from the Islamic world also began to visit England in the second half of the sixteenth century.[38] At yet another social level, N. I. Matar establishes that the first quarter of the seventeenth century saw Muslim prisoners in the custody of the sheriff Francis Bassett, who fussed, "How to dispose of the Turkes I have, I am in a maze."[39] As Matar notes, "although the separation between the two groups was frequently noted, English writers treated both Turks and Moors as a single religious and cultural Other."[40] Finally, Habib's research sheds light on African presence in not only cities but also the provinces, where, in one demographic model, white traders and Tudor elites purchased land and brought captive Africans to these regions.[41]

These records suggest that in the sixteenth century, non-white Muslim integration into England could inspire scenarios of entry into the transactional world of real estate and thus raise questions about legality and enforcement, both the provinces of the premodern sheriff. What, for example, did Lambert Waterson's designation as "denizen" mean in terms of possible land rights? What might it mean for a familial future that Peter Negro was able to leave assets to his son, even if these were movable goods and not real property?[42] What, meanwhile, might this testament reflect if Peter Negro was, as Folarin Shyllon suggested, possessed of "some African blood" but otherwise in identity a Spanish mercenary?[43] If, as Lynda E. Boose has argued, interracial reproduction engendered deep anxieties about racial and gender hierarchy, then how did such interracial unions, possible or real, map onto the regulation of land possession and inheritance rights?[44] Even when the answers to these questions are not fully calculable, one thread running through all these concerns was the enforcement of property rights for foreigners by the sheriff. In this period, a sheriff could, for example, seize the property "of any outlandish persons calling themselves Egyptians [Roma], that shall come into this Realme."[45] While this regulation referred to movable and not real property (at earlier moments fluid categories themselves), it intimates that the sheriff's deeply embedded historical relevance to questions about property extended in this period to the relationship between property and race.

—

It is within these contexts—pertaining to property, race, and policing—that the sixteenth-century morris dance lies. The sheriff's presentation of morris dance deploys a kinetic and visual language acknowledging the necessity of granting to non-white subjects access to certain elements of rights-based discourse while policing racialized persons' access to land possession and their ability to convey it to future generations. The Richmond pageant of the mountain and morris dance quoted earlier illustrates this point. Although this record does not describe

38
N. I. Matar, "Muslims in Seventeenth-Century England," *Journal of Islamic Studies* 8, no. 1 (1977): 73.

39
Matar, "Muslims in Seventeenth-Century England," 68.

40
Matar, "Muslims in Seventeenth-Century England," 64.

41
Habib, *Black Lives*, 194.

42
Habib, *Black Lives*, 301.

43
Folarin Shyllon, *Black People in Britain 1555–1833* (Oxford University Press, 1977), 8n2.

44
Lynda E. Boose, "The Getting of a Lawful Race," in *Woman, "Race," and Writing in the Early Modern Period*, ed. Margo Hendricks (Routledge, 1994), 35–54.

45
Michael Dalton, *Officium Vicecomitum: The Office and Authority of Sheriffs: Gathered out of the Statutes, and the Books of the Common Laws of this Kingdom*, rev. ed. (London, 1700), 81–82, in McGovern, *Tudor Sheriff*, 118.

Fig. 3 Wooden panel depicting morris dancers, c. 1580, oak, 15 × 69 cm, Lancaster Maritime Museum, LANLM.1969.43.1

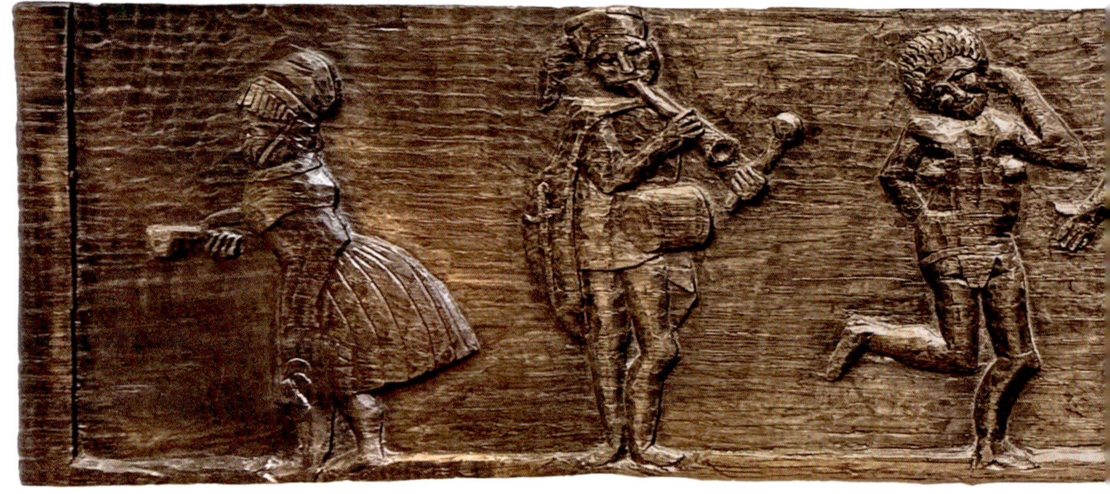

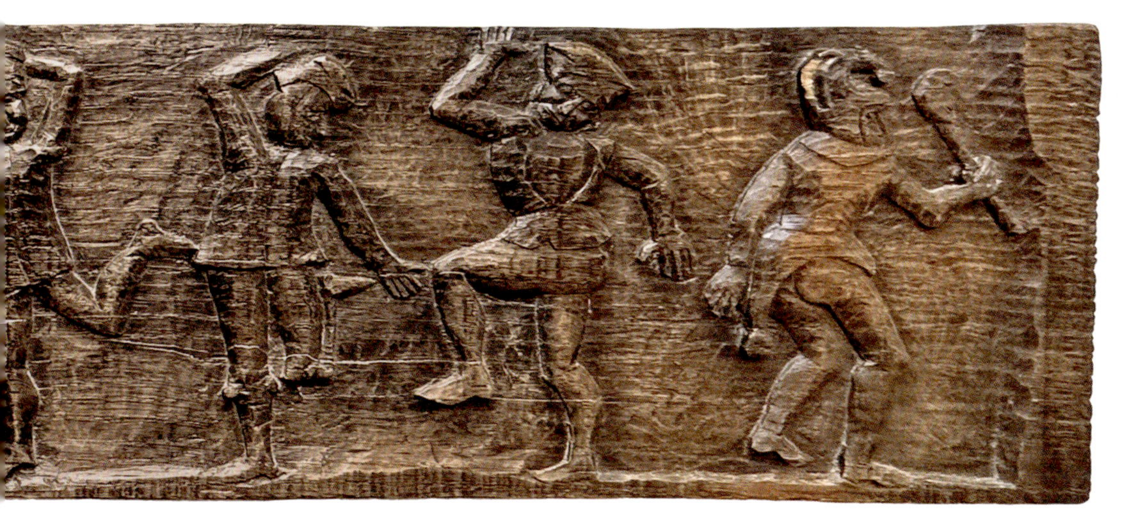

a sheriff's pageant, its explicit references to the dance and its performance before the king place it in similar categories of pageantry and political milieu. In addition, the unusual choreographic specificity of the Richmond account potentially illuminates what is politically, economically, and racially at stake in the less choreographically explicit record of civic and shrieval morris.

We might observe a number of important features in this example. On the one hand, the morris dancers' fresh, opulent trappings, their association with henchmen, their physical proximity to the king, and their symbolic reference to the Tudor dynasty all enter them into English political machinery. The emblematic Tudor rose costuming further invests the dancers in Englishness and thus potentially suggests their proximity to Englishness as an identity and set of rights. On the other hand, however, the mountain *entremet* and its visual motifs send a more complex message. As references to Henry VIII and Catherine of Aragon's union, the rose and pomegranate signal aspiration toward white reproduction to ensure perpetual white presence and dominance. The ornate mountain is also suggestive. Representing land and landscape, it communicates as such its high value, its gold and precious stones the riches that derive from the human management of the earth or, alternatively, the potential of land as a salable commodity and thus as a further guarantor of white lineal thriving.

This scene's choreography signals the restriction of racialized subjects' access to this land. As suggested above, even if the dancers' bodies do not impersonate racialized identity, racialization inhabits the choreography of morris itself, akin to what Ndiaye calls "the kinetic idiom of blackness."[46] Within that conceptual context, the morris dancers emerge from the mountain only to return to its interior. This choreography militates against their control or possession of the mountain. The morris dancers do not seem to stake out a place upon it; rather it subsumes them as they disappear into it, to be replaced

46 Ndiaye, *Scripts of Blackness*, 215.

by the end point of Christmas. If their steps are animated and vertical, this quality referred to as *ballon* in ballet nomenclature intends not to imprint the ground but to sustain the dancers' separation from it. Unlike the white Christian generational perpetuity to which the rose and pomegranate allude, then, the morris's blocking and movement quality signal for racialized subjects a consignment to ephemerality.

As a response to the scenario of African captives living in provinces where white traders were buying land and building new county seats, the morris dance that disappears into the mountainside comments upon the likely fate of certain non-white subjects in that landholding and landlording setting. As a vision responding to emerging evidence of non-white and non-Christian people ensconced in the urban economic landscape, the morris acknowledges one level of beneficial inclusion while drawing a line at land as a mechanism of futurity. Indeed, Habib's description of the records is striking precisely for its lack of inscribed futurity. Of John Blanke, the well-supported musician, we learn, "whom he married, and what happened to his family, is not archivally visible."[47] In the seventeenth century, not only did a sheriff incarcerate non-European Muslims, but also, upon some of these prisoners' eventual release, they were given no way home and left destitute in London.[48] If, in the sixteenth century, this brand of brutal process was too nascent to detect in the historical record, it might be reflected instead in the translucence and glitter of a shrievally presented masquerade—the morris dance that both acknowledged an increasingly integral Black, brown, and Muslim presence in England and, at the same time, choreographically and visually expressed the limits of this population's access to control over the ground they trod. In these ways, the sheriff's sixteenth-century morris asserts white futurity at the expense of all else.

As mentioned earlier, Ndiaye points out the importance of locating agency and mobilization to

47
Habib, *Black Lives*, 40.

48
Matar, "Muslims in Seventeenth-Century England," 69–70.

counteract European-made black dance's constant threat to demobilize. In her reading of the 1658 *Sir Francis Drake Revived*, which was produced by Sir William Davenant, "the transformation of Afro-diasporic war dances into 'Morisco' dance emolliates them by turning a kinesis of war into a kinesis of entertainment." Similar to the sheriff's morris in the previous century, Davenant's dance "allows [cimarrones] to assert their political mobility and simultaneously contains them."[49] In response, she directs us to acknowledge the Afro-Diasporic dancer and dancing master himself, the idea of "a member of a powerful confraternity bringing the art of Black formation to England."[50]

I conclude with another way to remobilize in the face of white artistic counterinsurgency, which is to target the sheriffs, the law enforcement officers who have always populated these accounts. Police still employ art as reformist strategy. When they paint their cruisers with Pride or kente cloth colors, they manufacture, as morris dance might, the illusion of unconstraint for racialized populations. The morris, however, exposes the fullness of what this illusion hides. Carceral art abets the requirement inexorably to claim space toward whiteness's perpetuity and its inherent landlording. To achieve, instead, a habitation of space informed by liberation, mutuality, and collective commitment to thriving demands the dismantling of shrieval and policing structures, including but not limited to their pageantry. The analysis of the sheriff's morris encourages us to seek beyond the legal, institutional pathways that Cheryl I. Harris's modern "whiteness as property" analysis offers.[51] In doing so, may we broaden the scale and raise the stakes of disruption until we have forced every cop, every sheriff—indeed the carceral state itself—to vanish under the mountain.

49
Ndiaye, *Scripts of Blackness*, 231.

50
Ndiaye, *Scripts of Blackness*, 232.

51
Cheryl I. Harris, "Whiteness as Property," *Harvard Law Review* 106, no. 8 (1993): 1788–1791.

On Removal and Preservation

Erhan Tamur

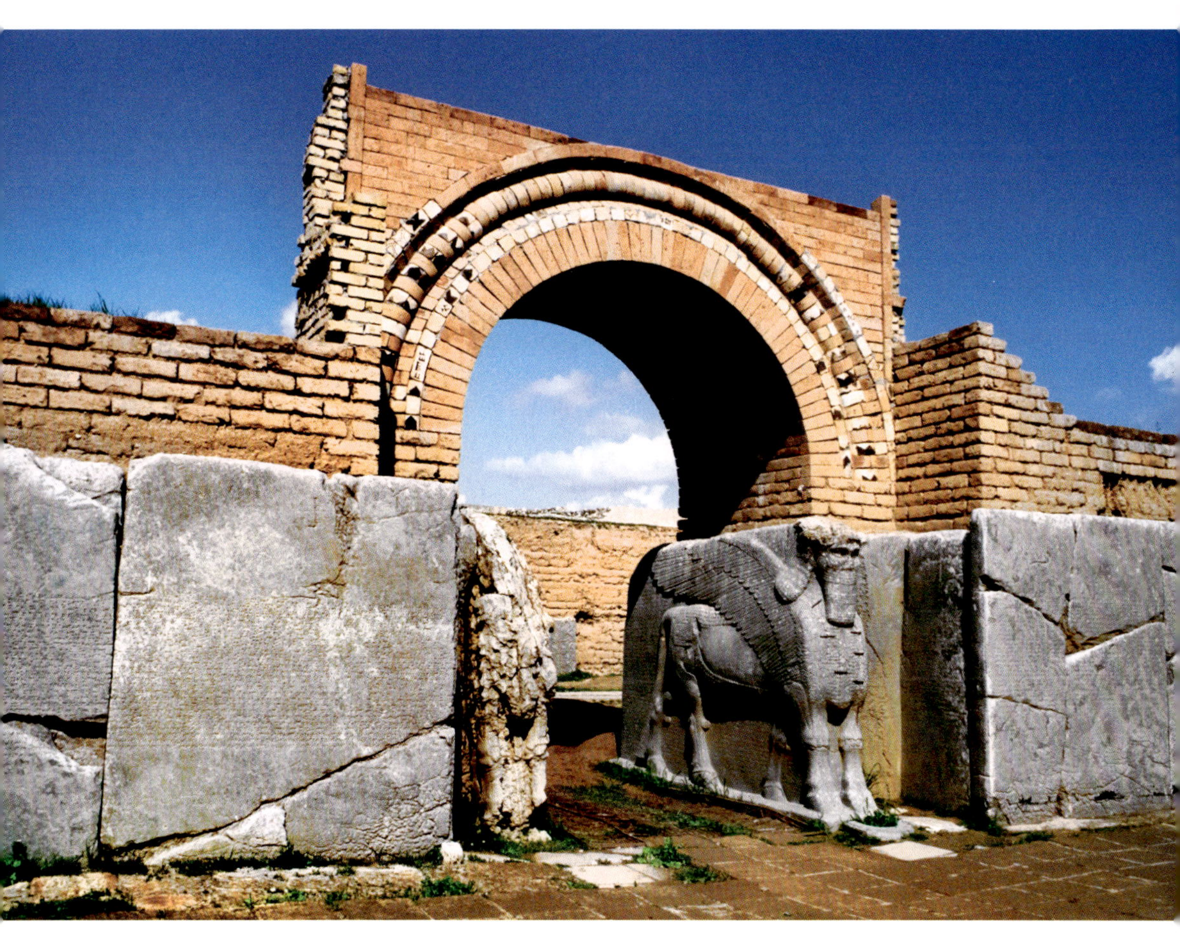

I determined, therefore, to saw the slabs containing double bas reliefs into two pieces, and to lighten them as much as possible by cutting from the back. The inscriptions being a mere repetition *of the same formula, I did not consider it necessary to* preserve *them, as they added to the weight.*
—Austen Henry Layard[1]

I would like to begin with a recent scene from a museum. Following the attacks by the Islamic State on the archaeological site of Nimrud in 2015, the Brooklyn Museum in New York revised the main wall text in its Assyrian galleries. Titled "How the Reliefs Came to Brooklyn," the new text concluded with the following statement:

> **Events in modern-day Iraq complicate how we talk about the *removal* of these reliefs from the site. Though generally there are those who argue that cultural heritage materials should not be transported away from their place of origin, the early *removal* of the Assyrian palace reliefs to museums in England and the United States has *preserved* them.... The Brooklyn Museum takes pride in *preserving* these antiquities for future generations of visitors.**[2]

← Fig. 1 Sculptures from Nimrud, Northwest Palace, Central Courtyard (Y), facing Door *f* into Room F, 9th century BCE, gypsum

Despite its self-congratulatory rhetoric that is void of any historical perspective on the relationship between antiquities and armed conflict, the juxtaposition of "removal" and "preservation" does raise an important issue. The former act enables and sustains the latter, echoing James Cuno's response to said attacks: "The world can only be grateful for the earlier regime of 'partage,' which allowed for the sharing of Assyrian antiquities with museums worldwide that could *preserve* them."[3]

Yet what were the conditions of the "removal" and "preservation" of ancient objects, and more specifically Assyrian reliefs? Rather than ascribing a timeless universality to these two terms, we must subject them to critical scrutiny, and that requires investigating the nineteenth-century excavation and acquisition contexts. In what follows, I take a closer look at the decision-making processes that went into the excavation, dispersal, and exhibition of Assyrian reliefs, which continue to have a profound impact on their reception today. Under the neutral facade of "removal" and "preservation" lie utterly destructive excavation practices and irreversible interventions to the materiality of the reliefs, the histories of which are either omitted or glossed over in public-facing displays and exhibition catalogs. Explicating such colonial contexts of "removal" and dispelling the illusions of "preservation" is central to any decolonial undertaking.

1
Austen Henry Layard, *A Popular Account of Discoveries at Nineveh* (London, 1852), 101 (emphasis mine).

2
Wall text, "How the Reliefs Came to Brooklyn," Brooklyn Museum, New York (emphasis mine). I thank Anne Dunn-Vaturi for providing me with a photograph of this wall text.

3
James Cuno, "To the Editor," *New York Times*, March 11, 2015 (emphasis mine).

Fig. 2 Nimrud, Northwest Palace, Room S, Slabs 19–23, with paint preserved on 21–22, photographed in December 1981 by John Russell, destroyed by the Islamic State in April 2015

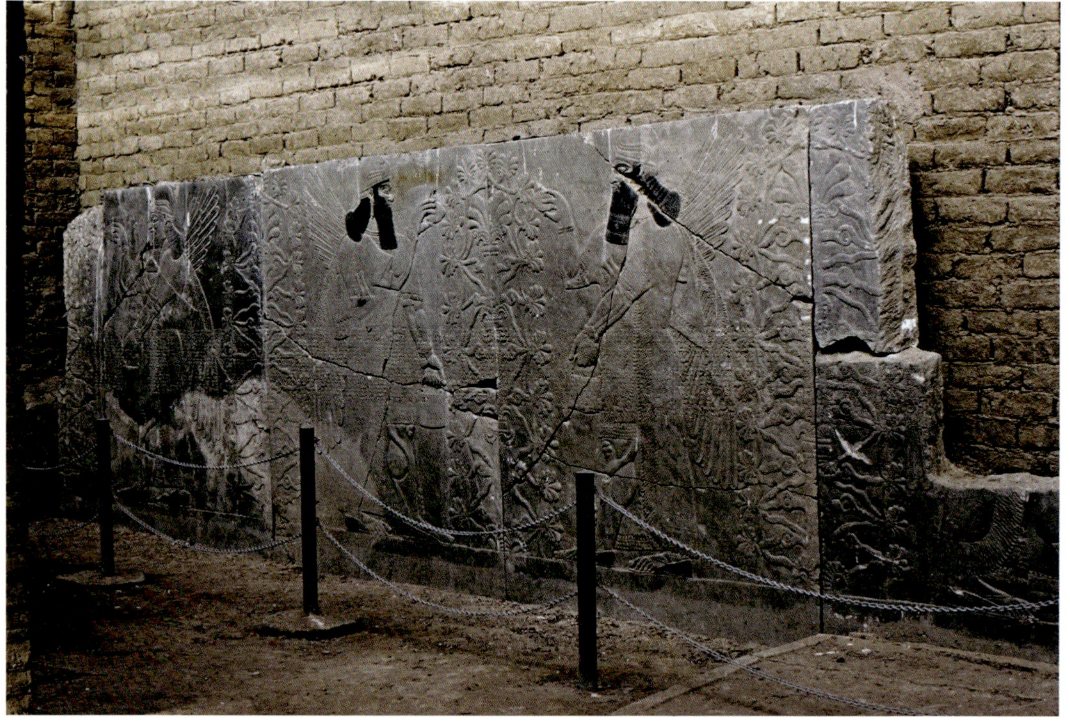

The Scramble for the Past

The beginnings of the modern discipline of ancient western Asian art history and archaeology are intertwined with histories of colonialism.[4] The large-scale excavation of the Assyrian sites of Nimrud, Nineveh, and Khorsabad in the 1840s were initiated by teams led by the French diplomat Paul-Émile Botta and the British traveler turned diplomat Austen Henry Layard. Over several decades, numerous private and public collections across the world came to be populated with Assyrian reliefs.

In their ancient contexts (ninth through seventh centuries BCE), Assyrian reliefs were part of meticulously planned architectural, ritual, and decorative programs associated with new building projects. Up to three meters (ten feet) high and about thirty centimeters (one foot) thick, these gypsum slabs lined the lower courses of mud-brick walls. Rather than structural elements, they were highly conspicuous architectural features, which worked in tandem with the portal colossi (human-headed lions and bulls) that were incorporated into gateways and played more structural roles (fig. 1).

Many of the slabs bore figural representations showing the king with courtiers and supernatural beings, performing rituals, hunting animals, leading military campaigns, and receiving tribute processions. Parts of the compositions were painted in black, red, blue, and white, which must have created a striking visual effect against the white background of the freshly cut gypsum (fig. 2). This visual complexity was further boosted by colorful wall paintings and glazed bricks, as well as now lost textiles and inlaid furniture.

The Writing on the Wall (and on Its Back)

The written word played an integral role in this overall scheme. An Akkadian text about the deeds of the king Ashurnasirpal II (r. 883–859 BCE) was repeated on every slab of his palace, either carved across figural representations or placed on a separate band between two pictorial

4
See Zainab Bahrani, "Conjuring Mesopotamia: Imaginative Geography and a World Past," in *Archaeology Under Fire*, ed. Lynn Meskell (Routledge, 1998), 159–174; Zainab Bahrani, *The Graven Image: Representation in Babylonia and Assyria* (University of Pennsylvania Press, 2003); Frederick Nathaniel Bohrer, *Orientalism and Visual Culture: Imagining Mesopotamia in Nineteenth Century Europe* (Cambridge University Press, 2003); Susan Pollock and Reinhard Bernbeck, eds., *Archaeologies of the Middle East: Critical Perspectives* (Blackwell, 2005); Zainab Bahrani, Zeynep Çelik, and Edhem Eldem, eds., *Scramble for the Past: A Story of Archaeology in the Ottoman Empire, 1753–1914* (SALT, 2011); Shawn Malley, *From Archaeology to Spectacle in Victorian Britain: The Case of Assyria, 1845–1854* (Ashgate, 2012); Zeynep Çelik, *About Antiquities: Politics of Archaeology in the Ottoman Empire* (University of Texas Press, 2016).

registers. Further, numerous uncarved slabs and pavement stones bore these inscriptions, and an abridged version was also inscribed on the backs of the slabs. These "slab back texts" would have been invisible to the ancient viewer and were intended for the gods.[5]

Now, let us read again the epigraph with which this essay begins. Layard notes how the stonecutters he employed sliced off the backs of the reliefs, describing the inscriptions as "mere repetition" while also justifying these practices as necessities of transportation: the inscriptions and backs "added to the weight." Placed at approximately the same height, the discarded "repetitive" inscriptions enveloped the viewer inside a space defined by the protective qualities of text and image. The continual repetition of the text, together with an emphasis on certain iconographical features—labeled as "monotonous" in some of the earlier scholarship—were integral elements of the ritual functioning of the space.[6] Additionally, the loss of these inscriptions and their insufficient publication have prevented scholars from an in-depth analysis of the relationship between architectural contexts and particular variants.[7]

5
John Malcolm Russell, *The Writing on the Wall: Studies in the Architectural Context of Late Assyrian Palace Inscriptions* (Eisenbrauns, 1999), 19–30.

6
For a discussion of the "monotony" of these artworks, see Georges Perrot and Charles Chipiez, *A History of Art in Chaldea and Assyria* (London, 1884), 107, 128, 286–288. On the role of repetition in ancient Mesopotamian art, see Zainab Bahrani, *The Infinite Image: Art, Time, and the Aesthetic Dimension in Antiquity* (Reaktion Books, 2014), 115–144.

7
On this issue, see Russell, *Writing on the Wall*, 30–33.

8
For example, a tiny fragment of a "slab back text" was recently sold at Christie's for $50,400: https://www.christies.com.cn/en/lot/lot-6411457.

9
See Julian Reade, "Restructuring the Assyrian Sculptures," in *Variatio Delectat. Iran und der Westen. Gedenkschrift für Peter Calmeyer*, ed. Reinhard Dittmann, Barthel Hrouda, Ulrike Löw, Paolo Matthiae, Ruth Mayer-Opificius, and Sabine Thürwächter (Ugarit-Verlag, 2000), 617.

10
On the base as a critical condition tying a sculpture to its place, see Rosalind Krauss, "Sculpture in the Expanded Field," *October* 8 (Spring 1979): 34.

11
Layard, *Popular Account*, 287 (emphasis mine).

12
See, e.g., Johann Joachim Winckelmann, "Thoughts on the Imitation of Greek Works in Painting and the Art of Sculpture," in *Johann Joachim Winckelmann on Art, Architecture, and Archaeology*, ed. David Carter (Camden House, 2013), 41; Georg Wilhelm Friedrich Hegel, *Aesthetics: Lectures on Fine Art*, trans. T. M. Knox (Oxford University Press, 1975), 2:723–730; Georg Wilhelm Friedrich Hegel, *The Philosophy of History;*

The widespread practice of slicing off the backs of the reliefs meant that hundreds of "slab back texts" were destroyed. There are only a handful of specimens in European and American museums, and fragments that occasionally resurface in private collections are sold at exorbitant sums.[8] Vital information about systems of fastening and toolmarks were also not adequately recorded, which at times leads to confusion about whether a dowel hole is ancient or modern.[9] Moreover, the decision not to "preserve" the bases, which were originally sunk into the floor and rested on a layer of bitumen to enable small adjustments, was key for the physical and conceptual "removal" of the reliefs from the site.[10] Indeed, it is worth exploring further what exactly preservation meant for Layard. Elsewhere, he writes:

> To lessen the weight of the lion and bull, without in any way *interfering with the sculpture*, I reduced the thickness and considerably diminished the bulk of the slabs, by cutting away as much as possible from the back, which being placed against a wall of sun-dried bricks, *was never meant to be seen*.[11]

The conceptual limits of "sculpture" imposed here betray Layard's privileging of figural content at the expense of every other aspect of the works' materiality. This attitude, together with the ideal of the harmony of "form" and "content," has a long history in Western art theory, and was part and parcel of the nineteenth-century engagement with ancient Mesopotamian art.[12] Accordingly, while Layard was disposing of inscriptions, backs, and bases on a large scale, he ensured that his workers "remember never to put matting in any position [during packing] where it may come into contact with the sculptured face of the slab as it marks the marble."[13]

Layard's justification that the discarded parts were "never meant to be seen" was not a recourse to indigenous ontologies—we have seen how critical such

The Philosophy of Right (Encyclopaedia Britannica, 1952), 266. Attention to symmetry, proportionality, and the harmony of form and content characterizes Layard's treatment of not only works of art and architecture, but also his ethnographic observations related to humans, animals, and landscapes. For example, see Austen Henry Layard, *Nineveh and Its Remains* (London, 1867), 92–93, 128, 211, 363, 369–70; Layard, *Discoveries Among the Ruins of Nineveh and Babylon* (New York, 1853), 7, 208, 218, 220, 255, 281.

13
Austen Henry Layard to Henry J. Ross, March 27, 1848, in John Malcolm Russell, *From Nineveh to New York: The Strange Story of the Assyrian Reliefs in the Metropolitan Museum and the Hidden Masterpiece at Canford School* (Yale University Press, 1997), 53–54.

"invisible" parts were in their ancient contexts—but an exercise of authority to determine what is worthy of the future viewer's gaze and appreciation. I will turn to the repercussions of this momentous decision in modern museum contexts later, but it suffices here to say that even the privileging of figural content did not ensure the "preservation" of all aspects related to it. For instance, although both Layard and the trustees of the British Museum supported retaining the traces of color on the reliefs, the slabs were nevertheless "dusted and washed" by museum employees.[14] Today, only minimal traces of paint remain visible.

Far from representing a universal ideal, "preservation" for Layard—and for most early excavators—was characterized by a set of exclusionary conditions that paved the way for what I call the domestication of Assyrian reliefs for a European and American audience. Stripped of their "hideous" masses and architectural qualities, they were essentially treated as two-dimensional pictorial surfaces. Frederick Bohrer argued that the publication and display of Assyrian reliefs reflect how "the distant Other is bent (if not broken) into a present sameness."[15] I would argue that this process should be traced back to the very act of excavation itself, the destructive nature of which inevitably negates any overarching claims of "preservation."

From Gifts to Commodities

The shipment of Assyrian reliefs to Europe, colorfully described and illustrated by Layard in his best sellers,[16] has been celebrated as a success story in numerous hagiographies and museum catalogs.[17] However, in addition to the forms of destruction mentioned earlier, hundreds of other sculptures were damaged during transportation, exposed to seawater and elements, or lost in transit.[18] The immense dispersal of Assyrian reliefs was also thanks to their utilization as gifts. Both Layard and the British consul general Henry Creswicke Rawlinson distributed pieces of

14
Julian Reade, "Nineteenth-Century Nimrud: Motivation, Orientation, Conservation," in *New Light on Nimrud: Proceedings of the Nimrud Conference 11th–13th March 2002*, ed. John E. Curtis, Henrietta McCall, Dominique Collon, and Lamia al-Gailani Werr (British Institute for the Study of Iraq, 2008), 15–16.

15
Frederick Bohrer, "The Times and Spaces of History: Representation, Assyria, and the British Museum," in *Museum Culture: Histories, Discourses, Spectacles*, ed. Daniel Sherman and Irit Rogoff (Routledge, 1994), 217.

16
See, for instance, the frontispieces of both volumes of Layard's *Nineveh and Its Remains* (New York, 1849).

17
Gordon Waterfield, *Layard of Nineveh* (John Murray, 1963); Robert Silverberg, *The Man Who Found Nineveh* (Holt, Rinehart and Winston, 1964). In addition to the Brooklyn Museum wall text mentioned

sculptures to friends, donors, and politicians. For instance, members of the Lynch family, who played a major role in steam navigation both locally and internationally, received Assyrian sculptures in return for their assistance in shipping.[19] Especially after the British Museum's 1854 decision to limit acquisitions to the "most remarkable" specimens, the reliefs that were considered "mere duplicates" primarily served this purpose.[20] While gift exchange fulfilled a critical role in sustaining harmony among the upper echelons of European society,[21] it did not operate entirely outside of the market, which brings me to the practices of an elusive but influential individual, Alexander Hector.

Hector's Razor

Alexander Hector was a British merchant who participated in the steamship surveys in Iraq in the 1830s.[22] Settling in Baghdad, he established a steamship line to England and carried out various commercial and political missions for Layard. He took an early interest in antiquities and visited Khorsabad in 1845, which had been excavated by French missions. Hence, crossing national boundaries in "a patriotic desire to secure to the nation

earlier, an older catalog of the Metropolitan Museum of Art states: "The walls of museums in many countries of the world attest to [Layard's] *successful removal* and transporting of these reliefs, first to India and then to Europe" (emphasis mine). Vaughn Emerson Crawford, Prudence Oliver Harper, and Holly Pittman, *Assyrian Reliefs and Ivories in the Metropolitan Museum of Art* (Metropolitan Museum of Art, 1980), 12.

18
See Julian Reade, "Assyrian Antiquities Lost in Translation," *Journal of Cuneiform Studies* 70 (2018): 167–188.

19
Geoffrey Turner, *The British Museum's Excavations at Nineveh, 1846–1855* (Brill, 2020), 205, 535–536.

20
Julian Reade, "Reflections on Layard's Archaeological Career," in *Austen Henry Layard tra l'Oriente e Venezia: Symposium internazionale, Venezia, 26–28 ottobre 1983*, ed. Frederick Mario Fales and Bernard Hickey (L'Erma di Bretschneider, 1987), 49.

21
On reciprocity and human relations, see Georg Simmel, *Philosophie des Geldes* (Verlag von Duncker & Humblot, 1900), 29–57, esp. 32–35; Marcel Mauss, *The Gift: The Form and Reason for Exchange in Archaic Societies*, trans. W. D. Halls (W. W. Norton, 1990).

22
On Hector, see Henry William Frederick Saggs, "Introduction," in Austen Henry Layard, *Nineveh and Its Remains* (Frederick A. Praeger, 1970), 41–42; Reade, "Assyrian Antiquities Lost in Translation," 174; Paul Collins, "From Mesopotamia to the Met: Two Assyrian Reliefs from the Palace of Sargon II," *Metropolitan Museum Journal* 47 (2012): 73–84; Daniel T. Potts, "The Lost Greek Epitaph from Harunabad (aka Shahabad, mod. Eslamabad-e Gharb), Iran, and Its Elusive Discoverer, 'Mr. H,'" *Ash-Sharq* 1, no. 2 (2017): 304–321; Erhan Tamur, "Of Consuls and Steamers: Material Foundations of Colonial Archaeology in Late Ottoman Iraq," *Journal of the Ottoman and Turkish Studies Association* 8, no. 1 (Summer 2021): 369–376.

Fig. 3 Collage of some of the Assyrian reliefs collected from Khorsabad by Alexander Hector

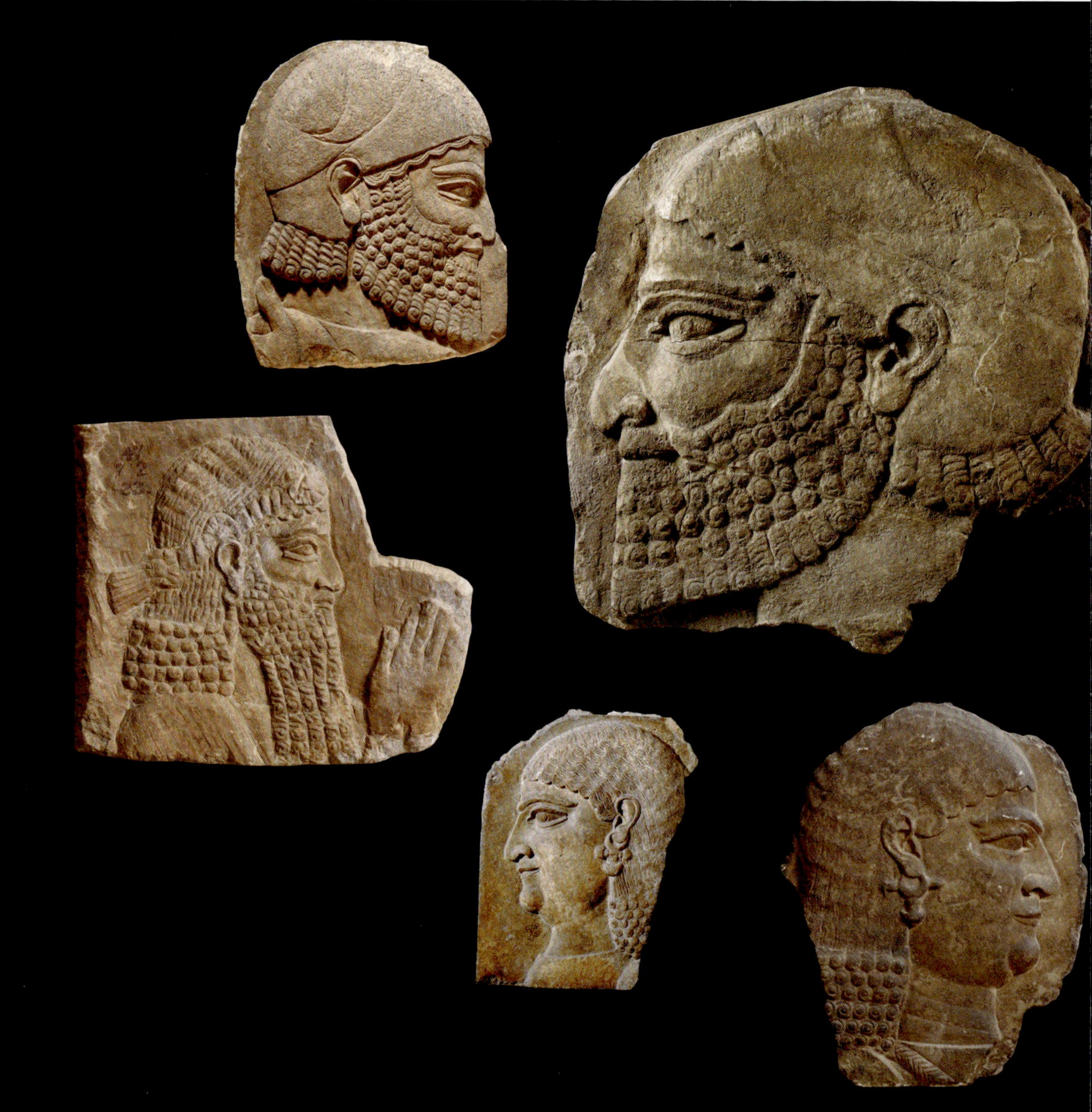

From top left, clockwise:

Wall panel, relief, gypsum, 710–705 BCE, 56.5 × 48.3 cm, The British Museum, BM 118818

Wall panel, relief, gypsum, 710–705 BCE, 58 × 53 × 10 cm, The British Museum, BM 118824

Wall panel, relief, gypsum, 710–705 BCE, h. 20.3 cm, The British Museum, BM 118810

Head of a beardless royal attendant, possibly a eunuch, c. 710–705 BCE, 56.7 × 56.8 × 10.3 cm, gypsum alabaster, The Metropolitan Museum of Art, Gift of John D. Rockefeller Jr., 1933, 33.16.2

Wall panel, relief, gypsum, 710–705 BCE, 53.3 × 45.7 cm, The British Museum, BM 118826

Wall panel, relief, gypsum, 710–705 BCE, 63.5 × 50.8 cm, The British Museum, BM 118811

Wall panel, relief, gypsum, 710–705 BCE, 160 × 121.9 × 22.8 cm, The British Museum, BM 118812

Wall panel, relief, gypsum, 710–705 BCE, 22.9 × 25.4 cm, The British Museum, BM 1847,0702.23

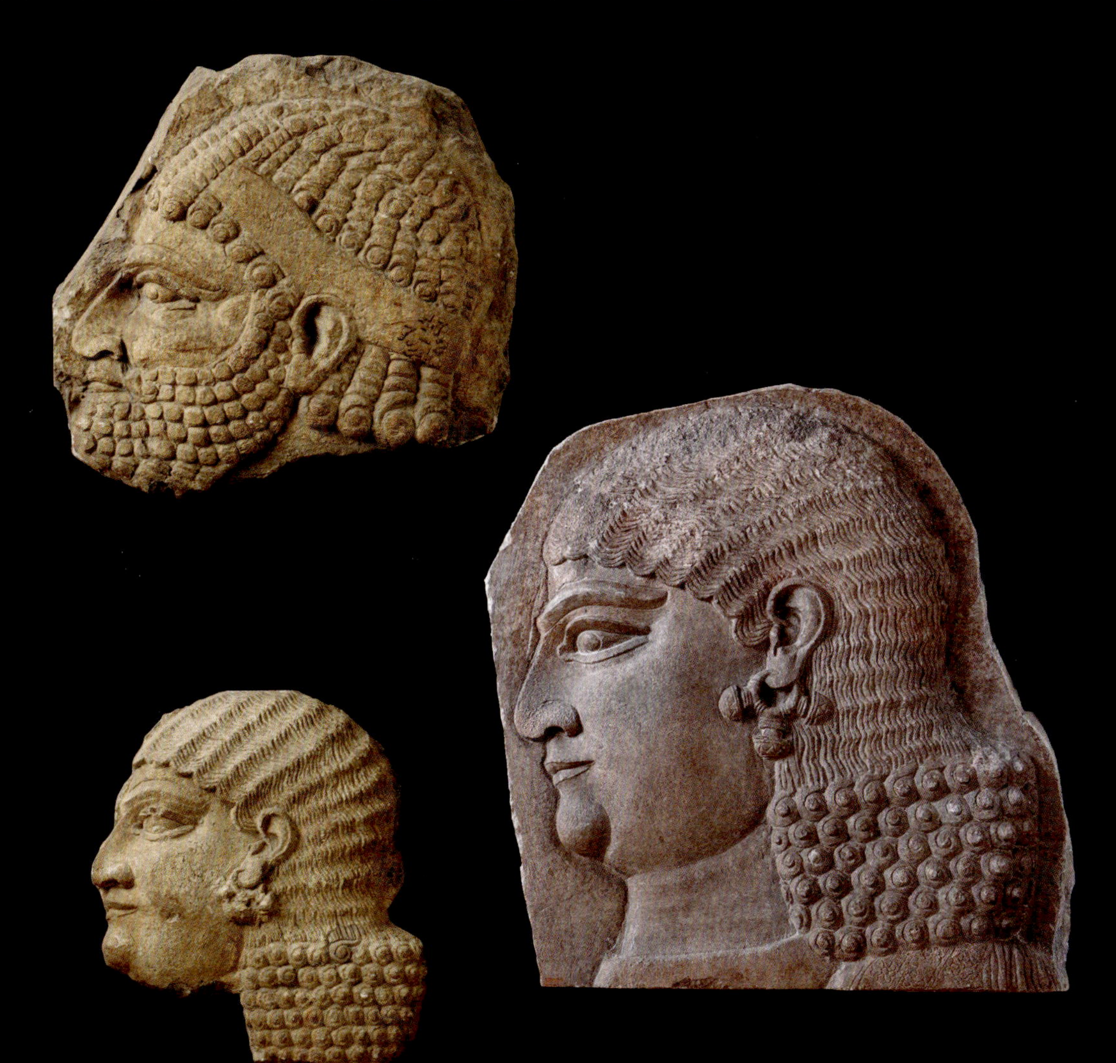

any relics or information of value,"[23] he wrote "the remaining sculptures looked very well and perfect while standing in their places, but fell to pieces immediately on attempting to disturb them."[24] He went on to "disturb" those sculptures by sawing off the faces of individual figures from larger compositions, which must have substantially damaged the rest of the slabs (fig. 3).

Informed by a fascination with the face as the seat of identity, this mutilation reduced architectural elements to individual portraits, with cuts closely following the contours of the head. A similar procedure, with neatly trimmed rectangular forms, was occasionally applied by others to pieces selected as gifts.[25] As for Hector's "portraits," some of them were indeed sent as gifts, ending up in the hands of figures such as British Prime Minister Robert Peel, while many others were sold by Hector to the British Museum—an acquisition widely publicized by the newspapers of the time.[26]

Layard's excavation permit was "in his name,"[27] and Hector's authority derived entirely from his personal relationship with Layard and Rawlinson.[28] Therefore, the rest of the Brooklyn Museum wall text quoted at the outset of this essay is not only incorrect as to the date of Layard's permit, but also imprecise concerning the provenance of those reliefs, which can be traced back to Hector.[29]

23 Joseph Bonomi, *Nineveh and Its Palaces* (London, 1857), 347, cited in Collins, "From Mesopotamia to the Met," 77.

24 Francis Rawdon Chesney, *The Expedition for the Survey of the Rivers Euphrates and Tigris, carried on by the order of the British Government in the years 1835, 1836, and 1837* (London, 1850), 2:136–137n2.

25 See, for example, two winged genies housed today at the Kimbell Art Museum in Texas (AP 1981.04 a,b) or numerous other pieces from Nimrud that eventually made their way to the British Museum (102401, 118899, 118900, 135156, 135157).

26 See Collins, "From Mesopotamia to the Met"; "The Nimrud Marbles at the British Museum—Second Arrival," *Illustrated London News*, August 28, 1847.

27 Austen Henry Layard, *Autobiography and Letters from His Childhood Until His Appointment as H.M. Ambassador at Madrid* (John Murray, 1903), 2:156.

28 It is clear that "Rawlinson named Alexander Hector as fourth in the order of 'precedence in disposing of the marbles.'" See Turner, *British Museum's Excavations at Nineveh*, 698.

The Third Dimension

Since museum didactics and displays are principal public-facing sources of object-specific and contextual information, they bear enormous responsibility for providing background for the "removal" and "preservation" of Assyrian reliefs. Yet most of the Assyrian reliefs displayed today are embedded into gallery walls to re-create their ancient architectural contexts in modern museum settings, which is regarded as part of the educational mission of these institutions. This aim goes hand in hand with a series of assumptions regarding the neutrality of cultural institutions, the authenticity of their displays, and the objectivity of their didactics. These assumptions might be lofty ideals, but are nothing but entrenched illusions.

The putative neutrality of cultural institutions has increasingly been questioned due to recent political events, but museums have *never* been neutral.[30] They were established within politically and economically stratified societies, and it should be stressed—even if it borders on the cliché—that museums not only *present* ancient artworks and worldviews but also *reproduce* them in the present. The form that this reproduction takes structures museums' claims of authenticity. This includes both the "authenticity" of the displayed objects (e.g., the attention paid to identifying forgeries) and providing an "authentic" experience for the visitor. For instance, at the British Museum, the discarded bands of inscriptions are made present through their absence in between the relief registers (fig. 4).[31] However, in almost all institutions that house Assyrian reliefs, the slabs that are displayed together come from different parts of ancient structures; given the absence of aforementioned ancient visual stimuli, it is impossible to draw any phenomenological parallels on the basis of "authenticity."[32]

As for the illusion of objectivity, notwithstanding the long-established philosophical objections to it, I regard it more as a practice of prioritizing content

29
Although Layard started his excavations in November 1845, his official permit arrived in Mosul only in late May 1846; Turner, *British Museum's Excavations at Nineveh*, 37. On the provenance of the Brooklyn Museum's reliefs, see Reade, "Assyrian Antiquities Lost in Translation," 174, with further references; Turner, *British Museum's Excavations at Nineveh*, 541.

30
For recent overviews of this debate, see Laura Raicovich, *Culture Strike: Art and Museums in an Age of Protest* (Verso, 2021), chap. 5; Robert R. Janes and Richard Sandell, eds., *Museum Activism* (Routledge, 2019), 8.

31
As of August 12, 2024, multilingual, partial translations of these inscriptions are being placed as didactics in between the registers.

32
Needless to say, we also have a clear separation between epistemology and ontology in European and American museum contexts and do not regard writing as constitutive of reality as ancient Assyrians did.

Fig. 4 Assyrian galleries at the British Museum, London

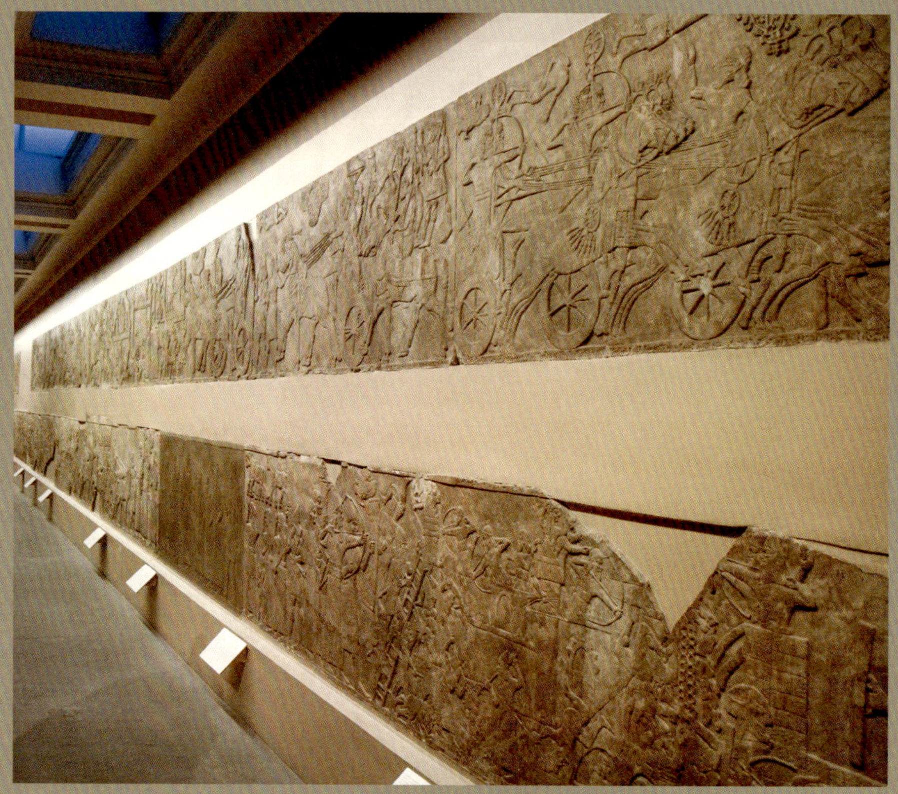

Fig. 5 An ancient Assyrian relief inside a modern wooden frame: Head of standing winged genie (*apkallu*), 883–858 BCE, gypseous limestone, 61 × 54 cm, Glencairn Museum, Bryn Athyn, Pennsylvania, 09.SP.1550

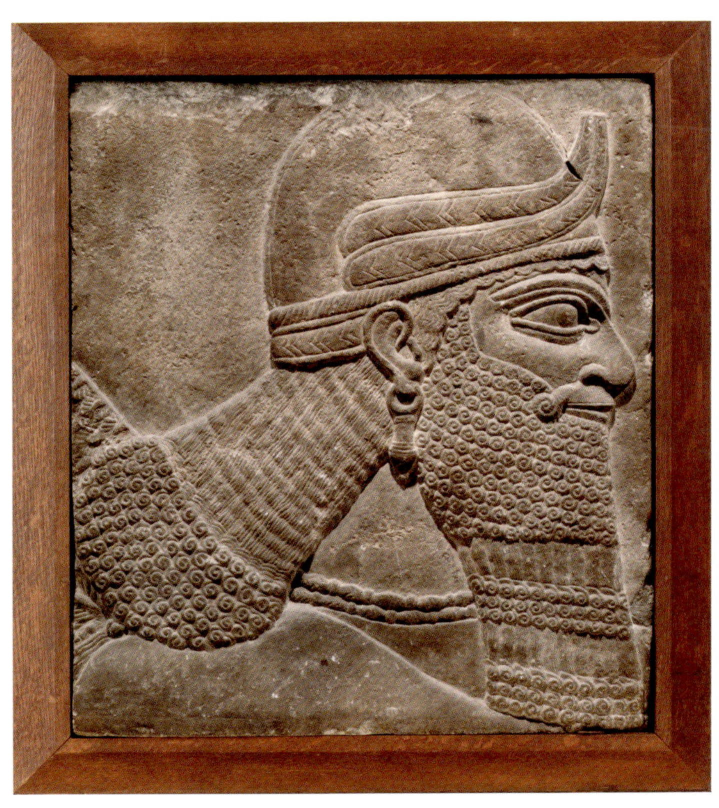

according to implicit or explicit ideological frameworks. For instance, if an ancient Assyrian relief is presented as a "portrait" inside a modern frame, I would argue that the process of "domestication" should be a primary concern in didactics rather than a sidenote related to provenance (fig. 5). Similarly, the occasional omission of the third dimension of Assyrian reliefs—depth—in survey books and museum catalogs[33] is not only due to its physical inaccessibility inside the museum walls, but also because generations of curatorial work have presented this state of affairs as the natural order of things. That their extant thickness is less than ten centimeters (four inches) and as low as two centimeters (13/16 of an inch) is a central story that cannot be glossed over by an exclusive emphasis on style and iconography. With their masses substantially reduced and their architectural qualities diminished, the Assyrian reliefs are shells of their former selves. Their exclusive display as embedded into the walls amounts to a curatorial operation that ultimately conceals the traces of their colonial excavation settings.

33
Eva Strommenger, *The Art of Mesopotamia* (Thames and Hudson, 1964); Winfried Orthmann, *Der Alte Orient* (Propyläen, 1975); Liane Jakob-Rost, *Das Vorderasiatische Museum, Staatliche Museen zu Berlin* (Philip von Zabern, 1992). The British Museum online catalog is not consistent; some entries provide information on the extant thickness, while many others do not (e.g., 124530, 124549, 124576, 135156).

—

What, then, is preventing us from pulling a few of them out of those walls and showing those surfaces that were "never meant to be seen"? I can already hear curators and conservators pointing to the costs and to the physical conditions of the reliefs, as their reduced thickness often threatens their structural integrity. But why omit this very fact from the museum didactics and maintain the illusion of "preservation"? What we can do in the here and now is to be honest with ourselves and the public about our curatorial practices, and to follow the threads that such an undertaking reveals about the colonial legacy of our discipline. Until then, museums are not in a position to claim moral superiority in times of armed conflict or to teach others what "removal" and "preservation" mean.

KEY TO ARTIST PROJECT

GLEXIS NOVOA

1
Castillo de Los Tres Reyes del Morro (Castle of the Three Kings of Morro), Havana, 1589

2
Edificio Bacardí (Bacardí Building), Havana, 1930

3
El Capitolio (The Capitol), Havana, 1929

7
Antonio Canova, after the Antique, *Winged Victory*, National Gallery of Art, Washington, DC, c. 1803/1806

8
Monumento a Las Víctimas del *Maine* (Monument to the Victims of the USS *Maine*), Havana, 1925

12
General Simón Bolívar Memorial, Washington, DC, 1959

13
Fuente de Neptuno (Fountain of Neptune), Havana, 1839

14
Angelo Zanelli, *El Trabajo* (*Work*), El Capitolio (The Capitol), Havana, 1929

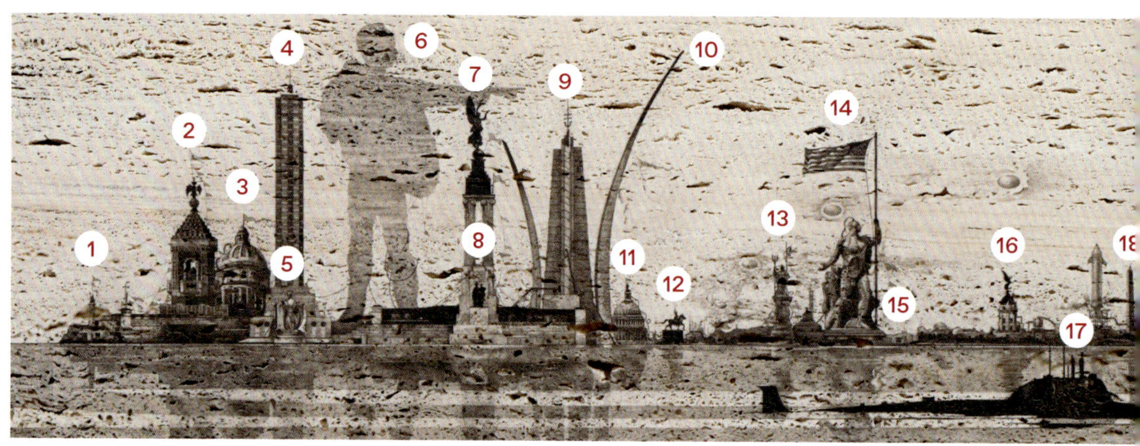

4
Obelisco de Marianao (Obelisk of Marianao), Havana, 1944

5
Gertrude Vanderbilt Whitney, *The Founders of the Daughters of the American Revolution*, Washington, DC, 1929

6
Tribuna Antiimperialista José Martí (José Martí Anti-Imperialist Platform), Havana, 2000

9
Plaza de la Revolución (Revolution Square), Havana, 1959

10
United States Air Force Memorial, Arlington, VA, 2006

11
United States Capitol, Washington, DC, 1800

15
Lincoln Memorial, Washington, DC, 1922

16
Niké (*Nike*), Gran Teatro de La Habana (Grand Theater of Havana), Havana, 1914

17
Kazan, Russian nuclear submarine, Havana, 2024

18
Washington Monument, Washington, DC, 1885

19
Cuban American Friendship Urn, Washington, DC, 1928

20
Emancipation Memorial, Washington, DC, 1876

21
Angelo Zanelli, *La Virtud Tutelar* (*The Tutelary Virtue*), El Capitolio (The Capitol), Havana, 1929

25
Monumento a Simón Bolívar (Simón Bolívar Monument), Havana, 1999

26
Edificio Martí o Mirador de Mantilla (Martí Building or Mantilla Viewpoint), Havana, 1958

29
Skyline of the Vedado district, Havana, 2024

30
Estatua a José Martí (José Martí Statue), Parque Central (Central Park), Havana, 1905

31
Christopher Columbus Memorial Fountain, Washington, DC, 1912

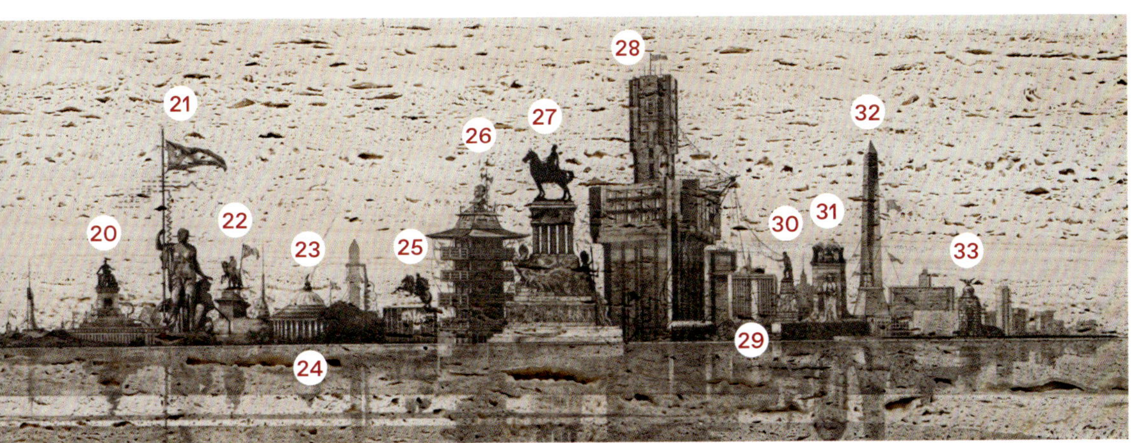

22
Major General George B. McClellan Statue, Washington, DC, 1907

23
El Mercurio (*Mercury*), Lonja del Comercio (Trade Market), Havana, 1909

24
Thomas Jefferson Memorial, Washington, DC, 1943

27
Monumento a Máximo Gómez (Máximo Gómez Monument), Havana, 1935

28
Embassy of Russia, Havana, 1987

32
Obelisk dedicated to Rear Admiral Andrew Dunlap III, Arlington National Cemetery, Arlington, VA, 1914

33
Clarendon War Memorial, Arlington, VA, 1931

Seeta Chaganti is a professor of English at the University of California, Davis. Her current project traces the history of the sheriff, from pre-Conquest England to the modern United States, as evidence supporting the abolition of police. Her 2018 book *Strange Footing* won the Modern Language Association's Aldo and Jeanne Scaglione Prize for Comparative Literary Studies.

Lisa Gail Collins is Professor of Art on the Sarah Gibson Blanding Chair and Director of the American Studies Program at Vassar College. She received her BA in art history from Dartmouth College and her PhD in American Studies from University of Minnesota. Her latest book, *Stitching Love and Loss: A Gee's Bend Quilt*—a meditation on suffering, creativity, resilience, and grace—was awarded the 2023 Horowitz Book Prize by Bard Graduate Center.

Lorraine Mendes is a Brazilian researcher and curator at the Pinacoteca de São Paulo. She is a PhD candidate in art history and criticism at the Universidade Federal do Rio de Janeiro, and has curated exhibitions such as *Dos Brasis: Arte e pensamento negro* (*Dos Brasis—Black Art, Black Thinking*, 2023–2024) and artist Rosana Paulino's *Time of Things* (2022) at Mendes Wood DM in Brussels.

Wanda Nanibush is an Anishinaabe-kwe image and word warrior, curator, and community organizer from Beausoleil First Nation. Based in Toronto, Nanibush is the founding director of aabaakwad, an international yearly gathering of Indigenous curators, writers, and artists that last took place at the Venice Biennale. She recently won the Toronto Book Award for her coauthored volume *Moving the Museum*, which chronicles some of her groundbreaking work at the Art Gallery of Ontario as the inaugural curator of Indigenous art.

Glexis Novoa was a key participant in the vibrant art scene known as the renaissance of Cuban art in the 1980s. He was the founder of the Grupo Provisional, a pioneer of performance, political activism, and collectivist practices. Residing in Miami since 1995, Novoa is recognized for his site-specific wall drawings, which exist on the border between ephemeral art and architecture.

Juno Richards is associate professor of English and Women, Gender, and Sexuality Studies at Yale University. They are the author of *The Fury Archives: Female Citizenship, Human Rights, and the International Avant-Gardes* and coauthor of *The Ferrante Letters: An Experiment in Collective Criticism*.

Igor Simões is an independent curator and adjunct professor of history, theory, and art criticism, as well as methodology and practice in art teaching, at the Universidade Estadual do Rio Grande do Sul. He served as curator of *Dos Brasis: Arte e pensamento negro* (*Dos Brasis—Black Art, Black Thinking*, 2023–2024), and his research focuses on the intersections of histories of art and racialization in Brazilian art.

Erhan Tamur is a lecturer at the University of York. After receiving his PhD from Columbia University, he worked at the Morgan Library & Museum and the Metropolitan Museum of Art. His publications have focused on archaeological and art historical theory, the politics of archaeology, and ancient western Asian art.

INDEX

Numbers in **boldface** refer to illustrations.

IMAGE CREDITS

Cover, pages 4–5, 33, 34–35, 148–149, insert, © Glexis Novoa; photo: Oriol Tarridas Photography

"where tenderness is possible"
page 19, photo: Erika deVries; page 20, photo: Becky Cote; pages 25, 26–27, photos: Zola Simone Sullivan

"Arts of Reckoning"
fig. 1, photo: Courtesy of Rare Book and Special Collections, Library of Congress, Washington, DC; fig. 2, © Tate; fig. 3, Courtesy of the artist; fig. 4, © 2026 Mickalene Thomas / Artists Rights Society (ARS), New York; fig. 5, courtesy of Janus Films

"This Performer Is Not an Artifact"
page 63, photo: Michael Beynon; figs. 1, 3, © Estate of James Luna; photo: Courtesy of the Estate of James Luna and Garth Greenan Gallery, New York; fig. 2, photo: William Lindsay, from J. David Galway, *Chronicle Journal*, January 13, 1988; fig. 4, photo: Michael Beynon

"'I refuse': Estevão Silva"
figs. 1, 5, Acervo Museu Nacional de Belas Artes; figs. 2, 4, photo: Romulo Fialdini/Tempo Composto; figs. 3, 6, photo: Isabella Matheus

"Pageantry as Police Work"
page 107, © Victoria and Albert Museum, London; figs. 1, 2, photo: G. Adler, E. Jank; fig. 3, Copyright Lancaster Maritime Museum

"On Removal and Preservation"
fig. 1, photo: Mick Sharp / Alamy Stock Photo; fig. 2, photo: John Russell; fig. 3 (all but image on far right), © The Trustees of the British Museum; fig. 4, photo: Erhan Tamur, 2015

This volume was published by the Center for Advanced Study in the Visual Arts and the Office of Brand Strategy and Publishing at the National Gallery of Art.

nga.gov

Brand Strategy and Publishing

Chief Brand Officer and Publisher
Peggy Martin

Managing Editor
Emily Zoss

Project Editor
Magda Nakassis

Design Manager
Brad Ireland

Production Manager
Christina Wiginton

Production Associate
Jasmine Lee

Production Assistant
Mariah Shay

Copyediting by Magda Nakassis
Design by Extra Official, Elizabeth Azen Andia and Caleb Kozlowski
Proofreading by Katie Brennan
Indexing by Kathleen Friello
Rights clearance by Gary Calcagno

All translations from non-English-language editions are the author's own unless otherwise indicated. Steve Berg translated "'I refuse': Estevão Silva" from Portuguese.

Typeset in Firs Neue (TypeType), Favorit (Dinamo), and Dashiell (Adobe)

Paper
Fedrigoni Sirio Perla and GardaPat Kiara

Printed by
Verona Libri, Italy

Distributed by Yale University Press, New Haven and London
yalebooks.com/art

Authorized Representative in the EU: Easy Access System Europe, Mustamäe tee 50, 10621 Tallinn, Estonia, gpsr.requests@easproject.com

Library of Congress Control Number: 2025945253
ISBN: 978-0-300-29038-7 (paperback)
ISBN: 978-0-300-29040-0 (ebook)
ISSN: 3068-8957 (print)
ISSN: 3068-8922 (online)

Art &
Volume 1

Illustration details
cover, pages 4–5, 33, 148–149: Glexis Novoa, *Art & Histories, Havana-Washington Island*, 2024, graphite on travertine marble, 45.7 × 121.9 cm

10 9 8 7 6 5 4 3 2 1

Detachable insert
Unfold with care

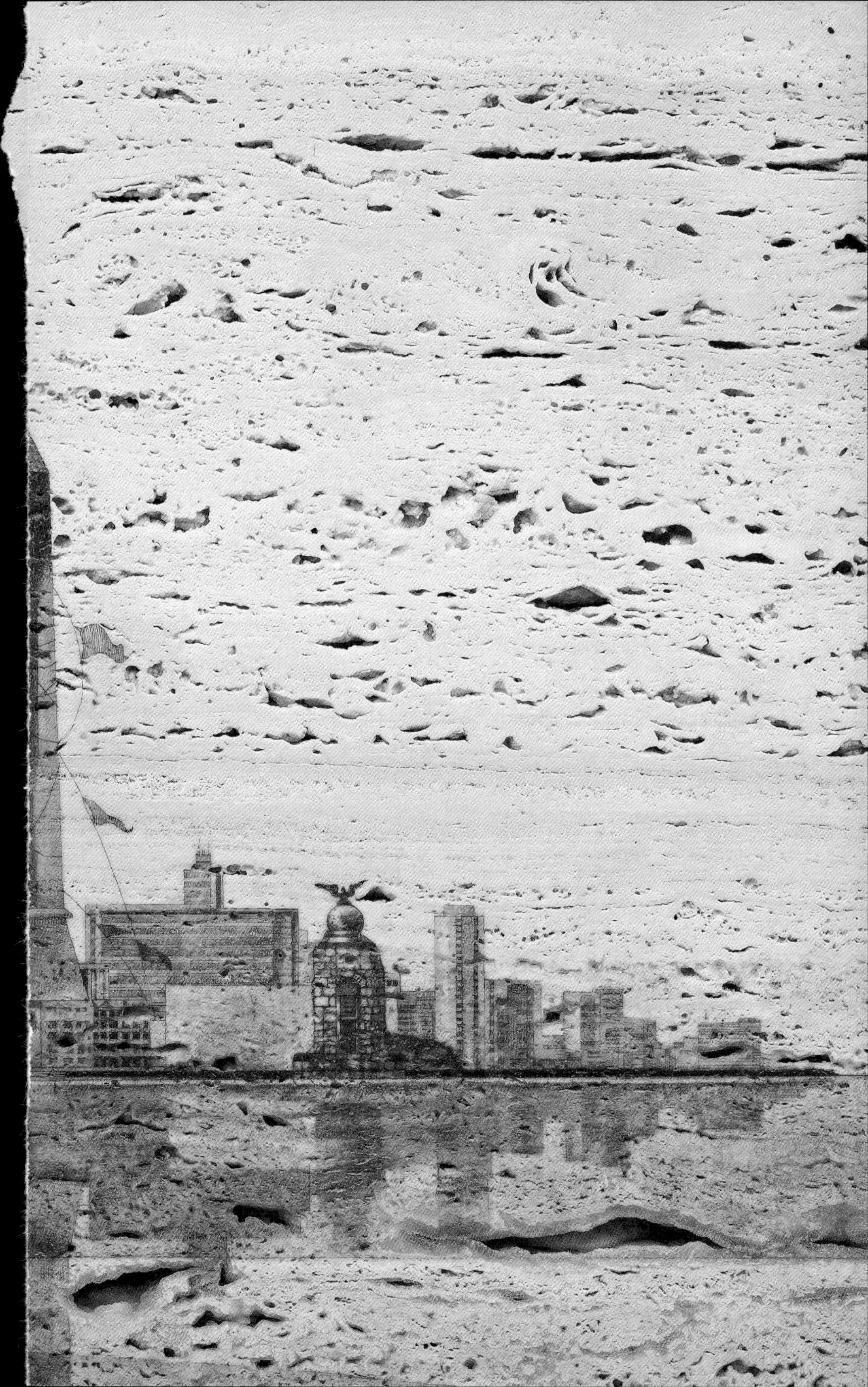

Glexis Novoa, *Art & Histories, Havana-Washington Island* (detail), 2024, graphite on travertine marble, 45.7 × 121.9 cm. © Glexis Novoa

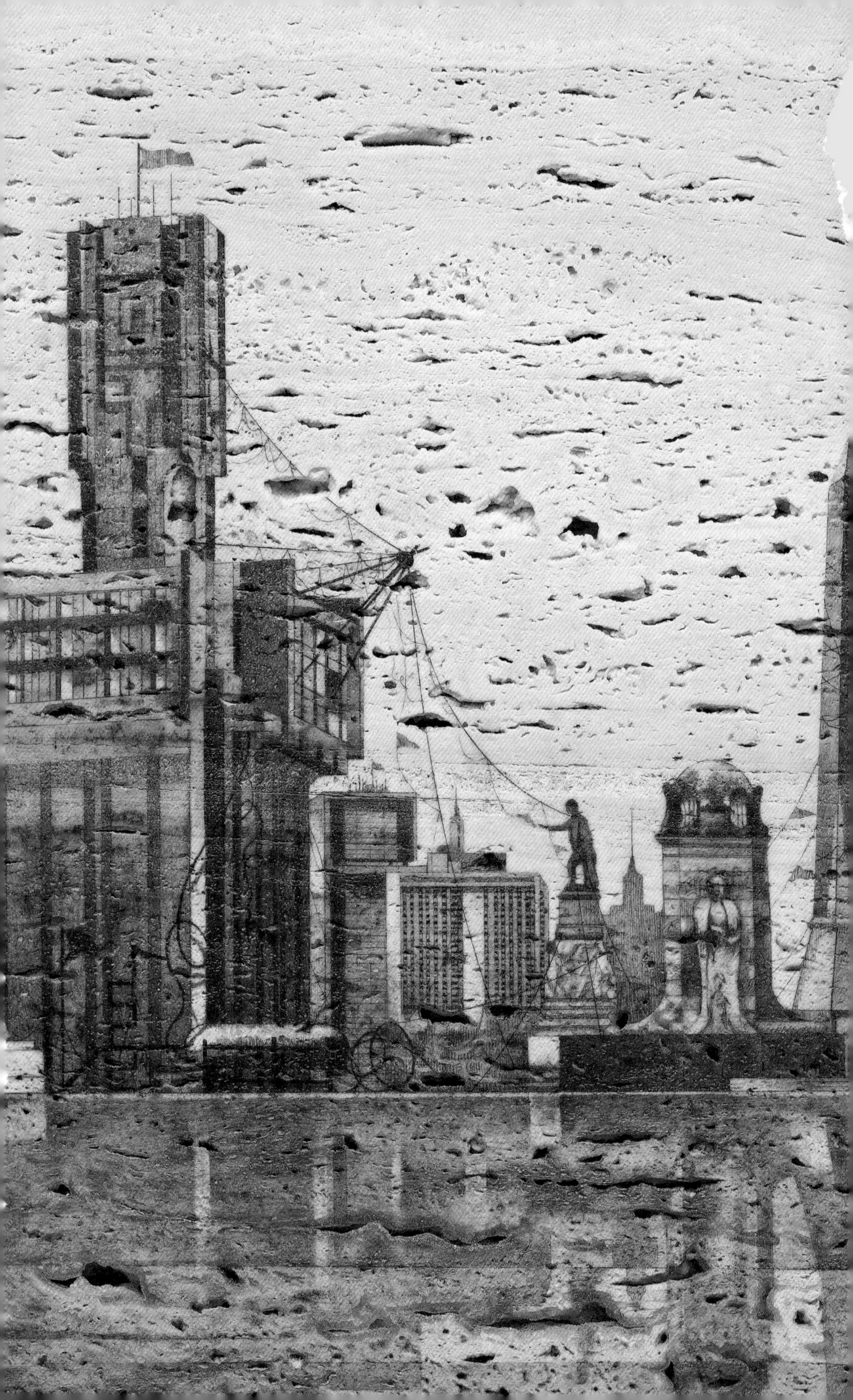

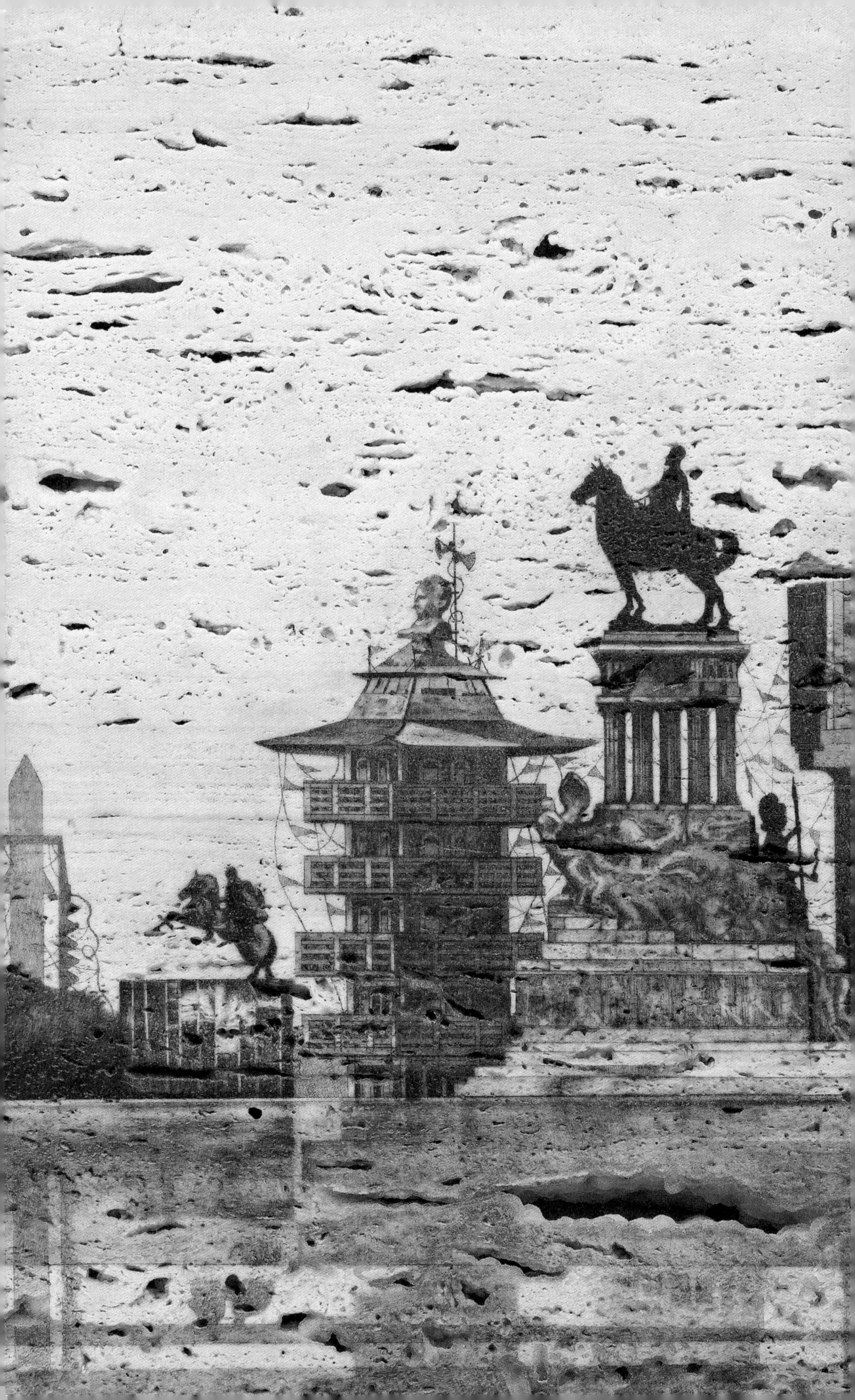

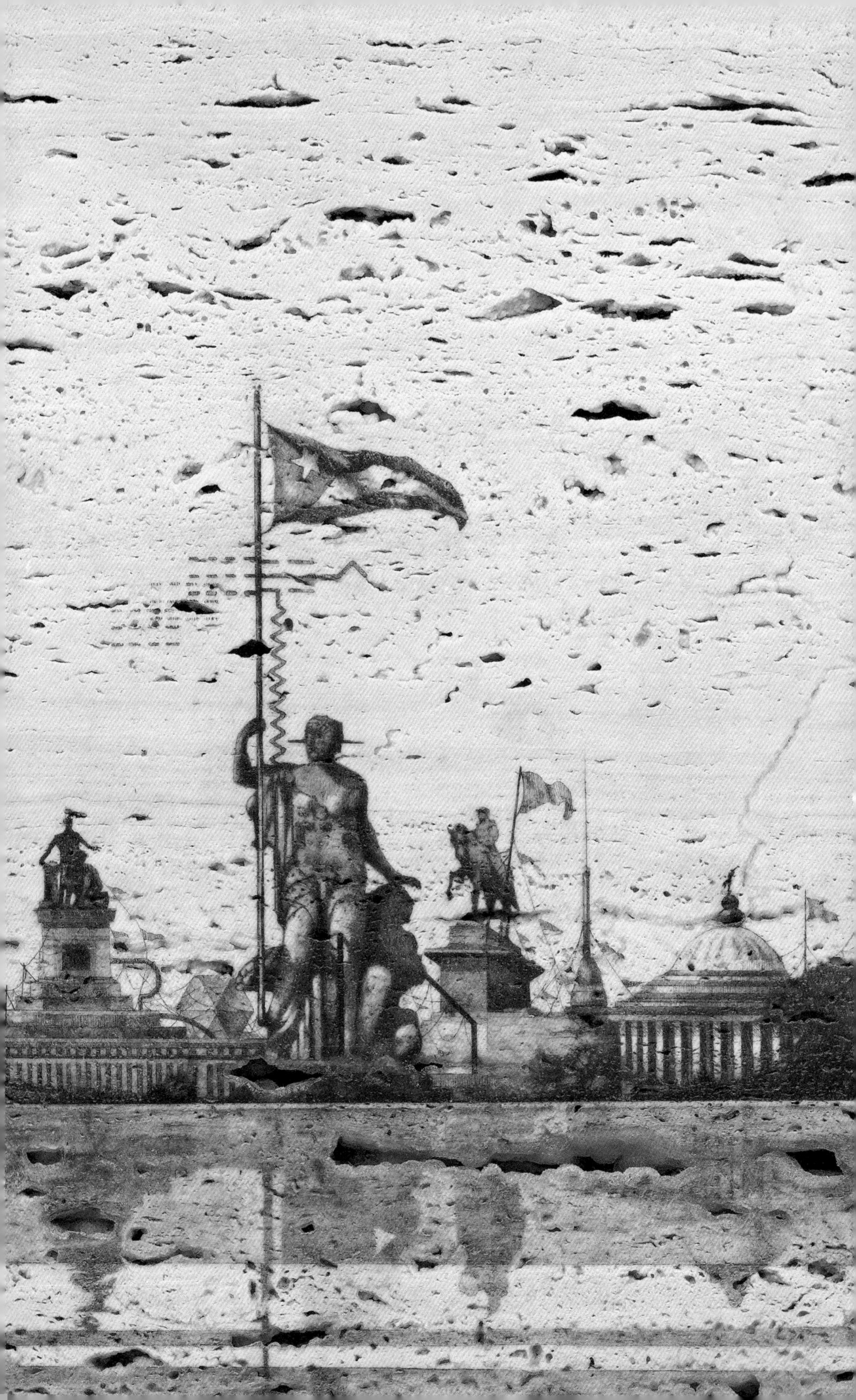

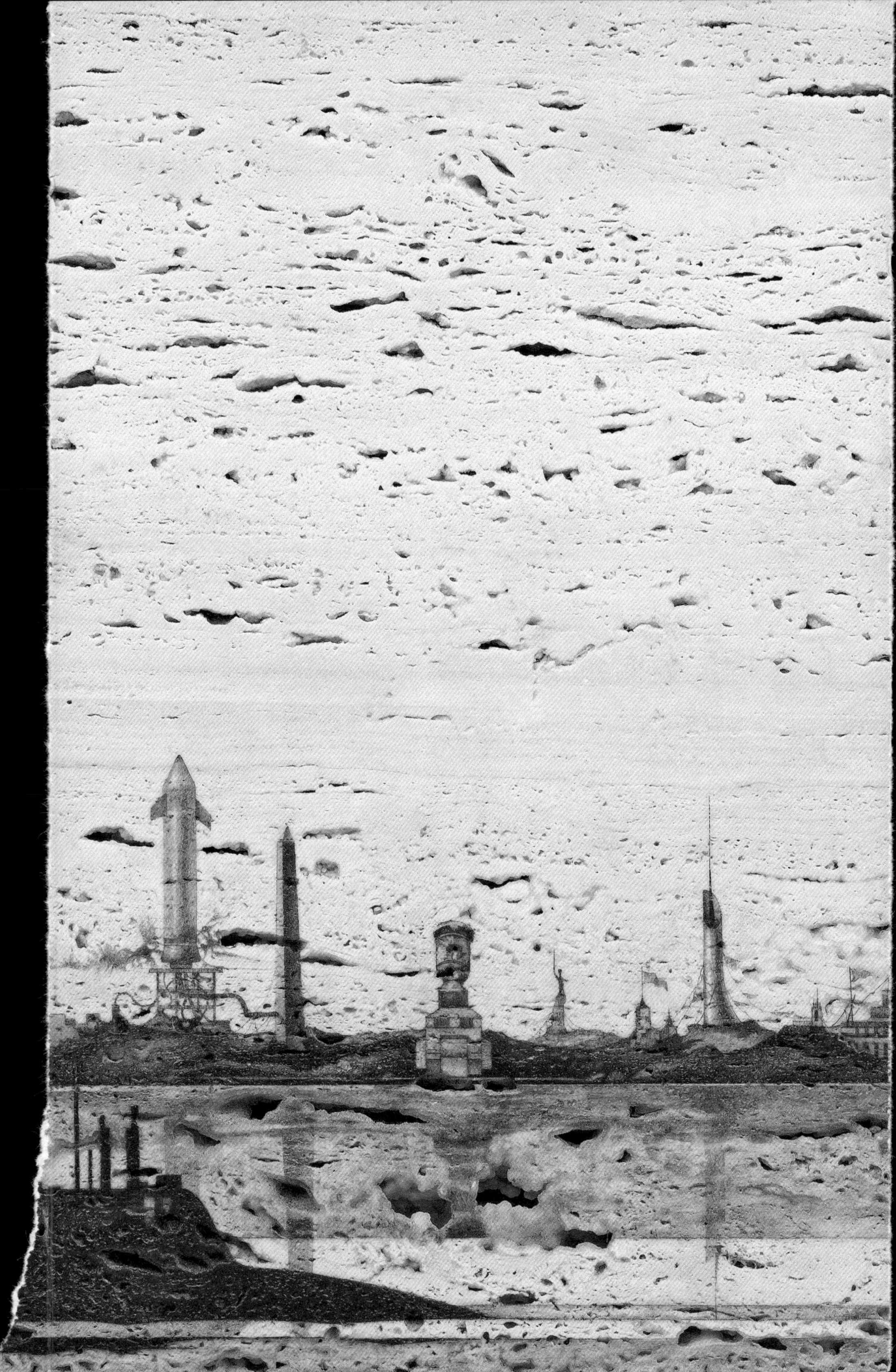

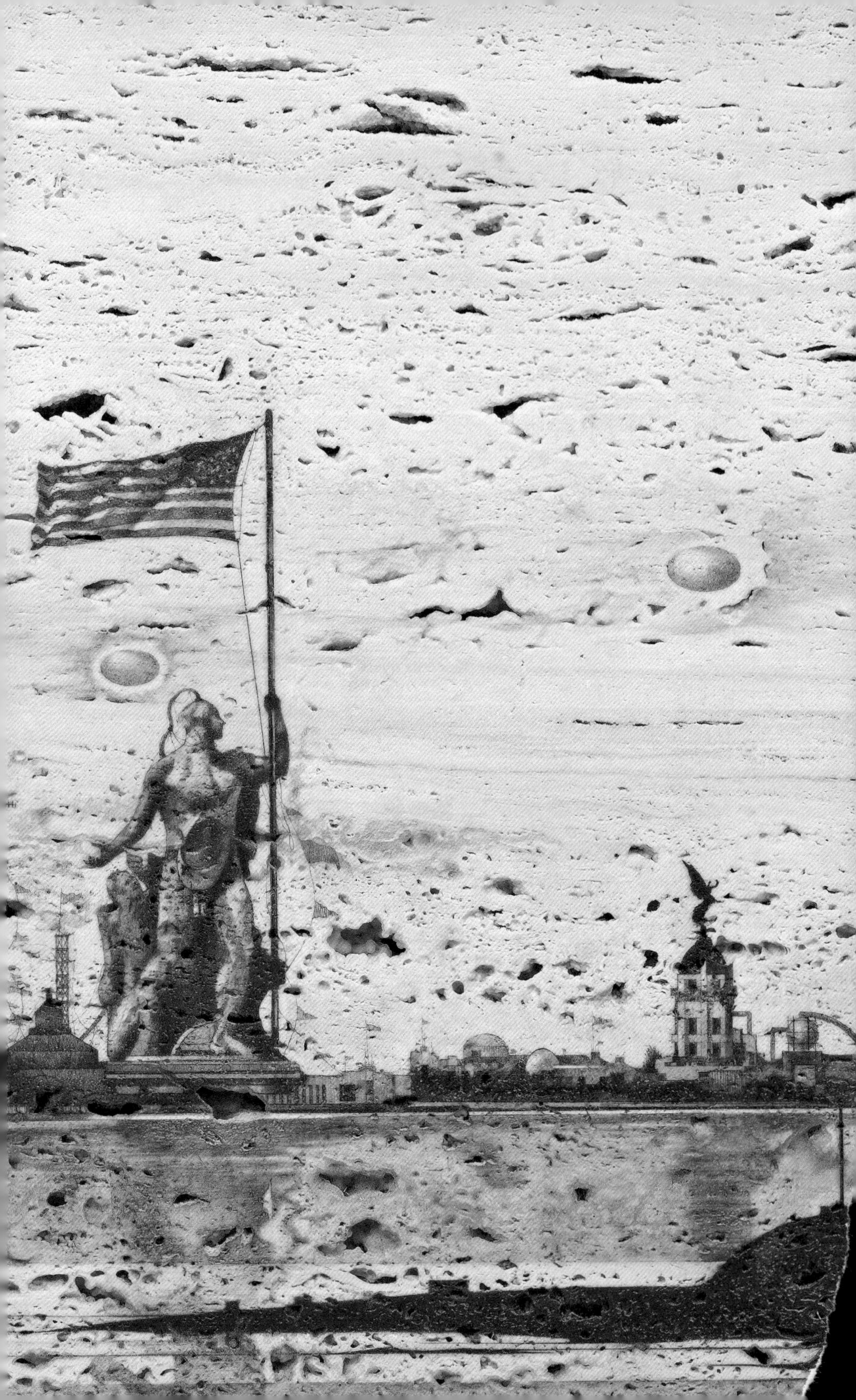

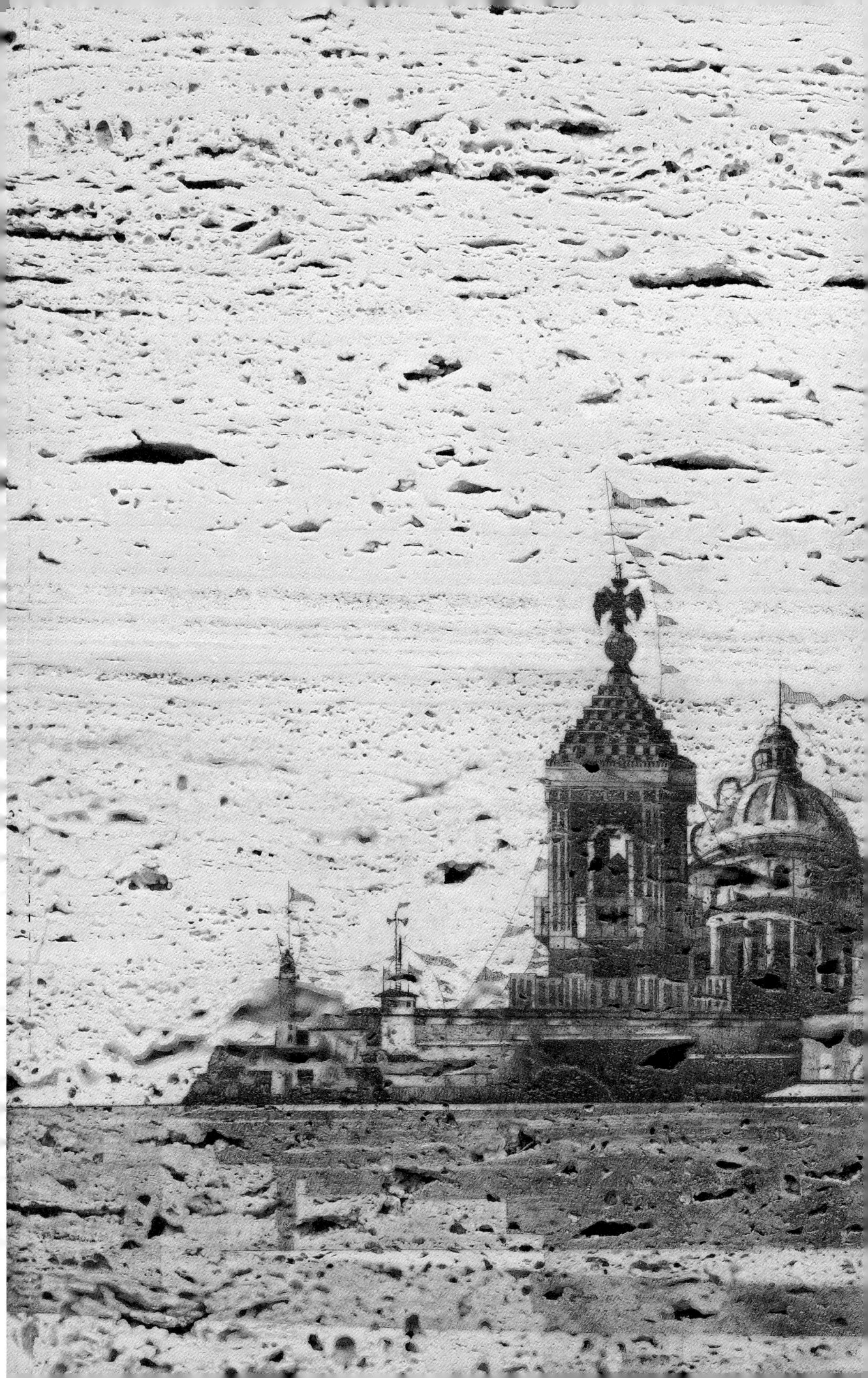

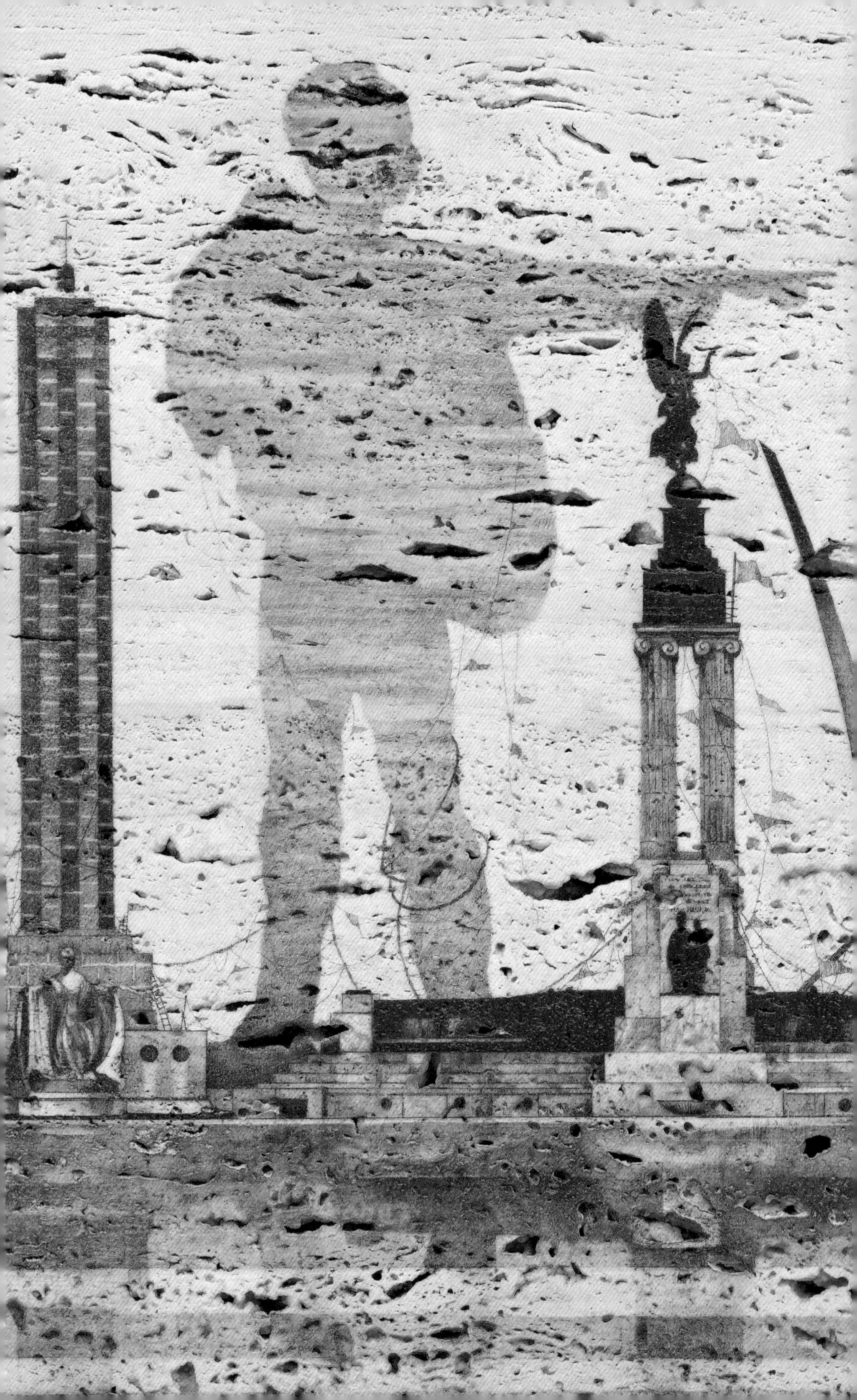

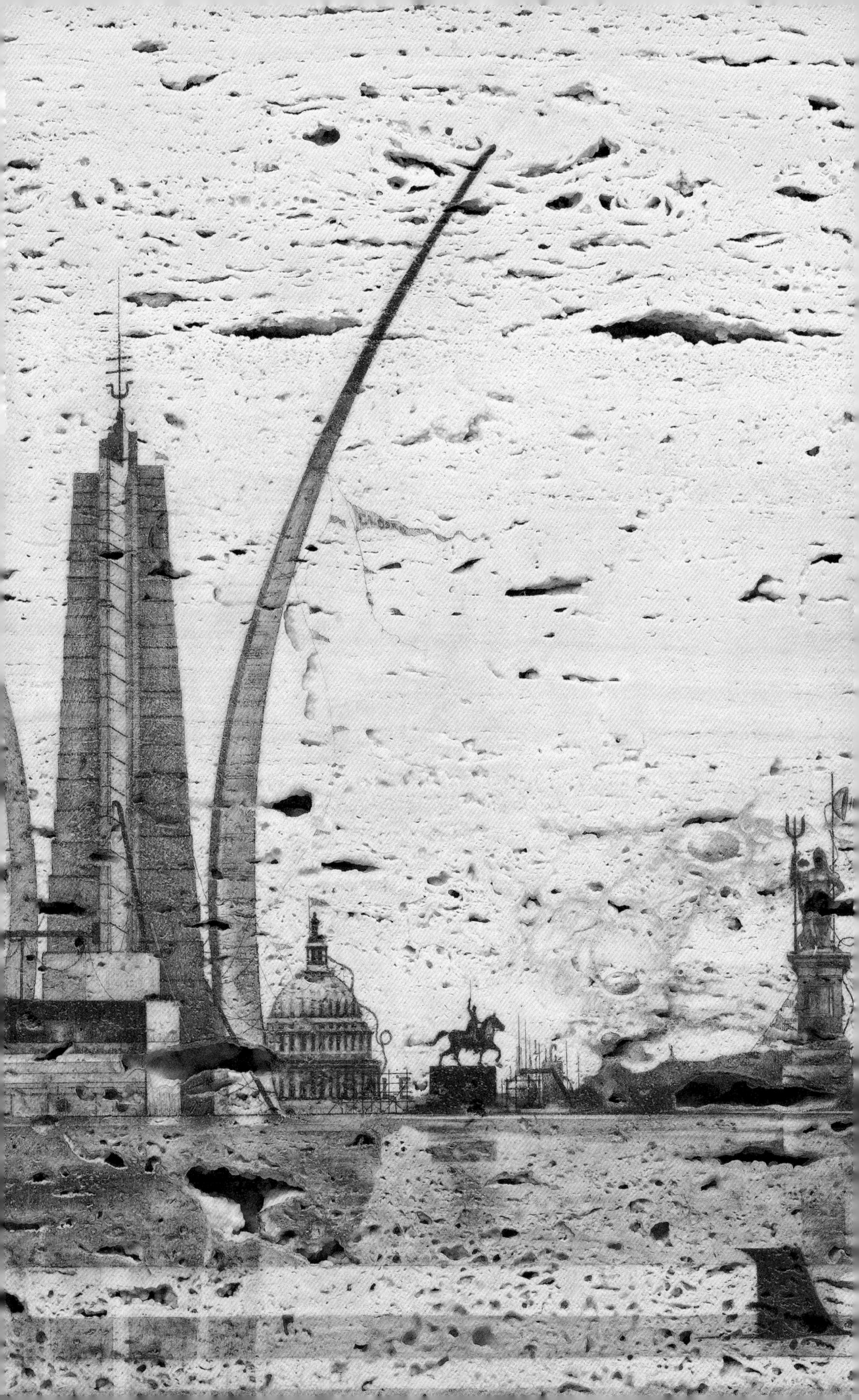

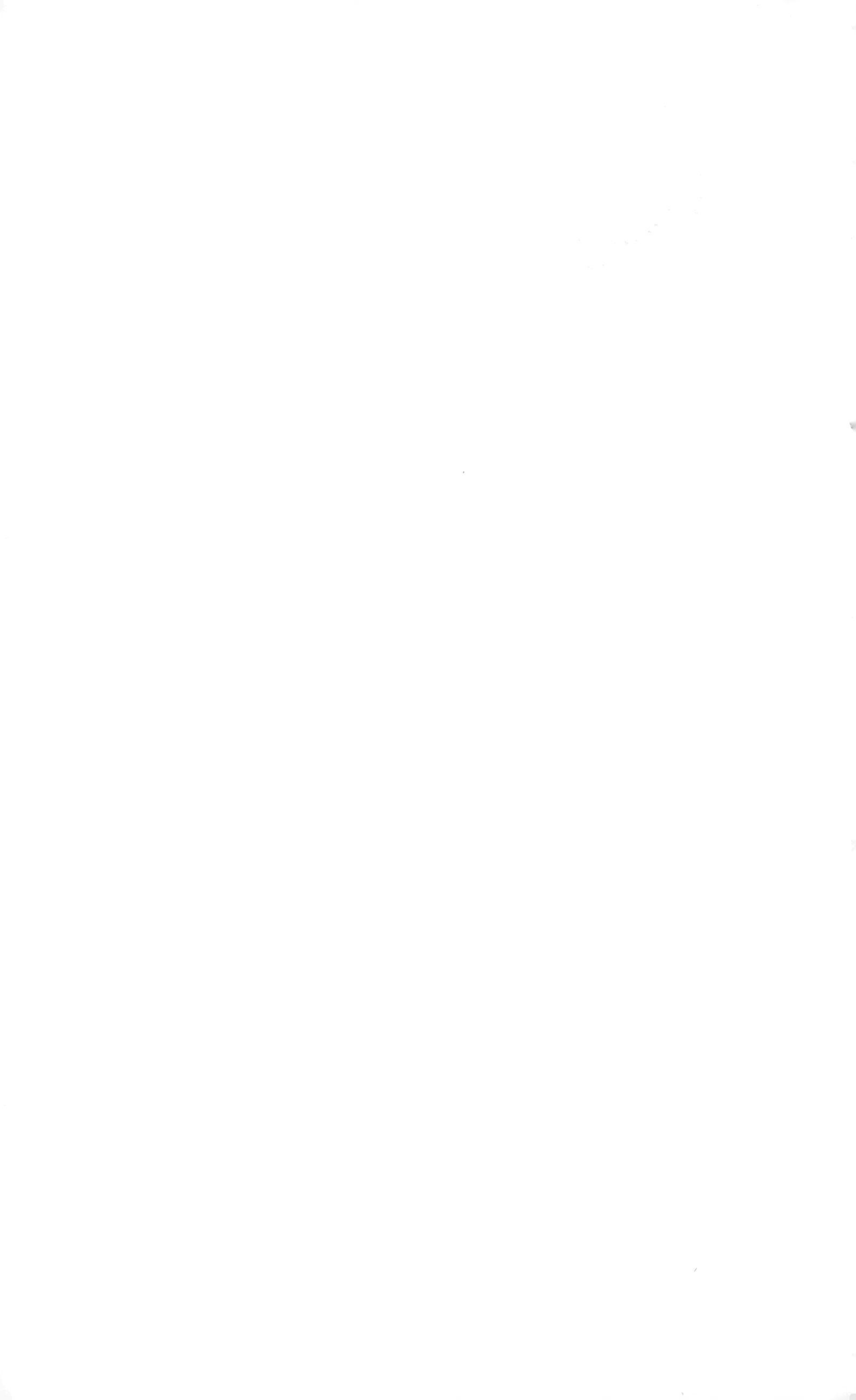